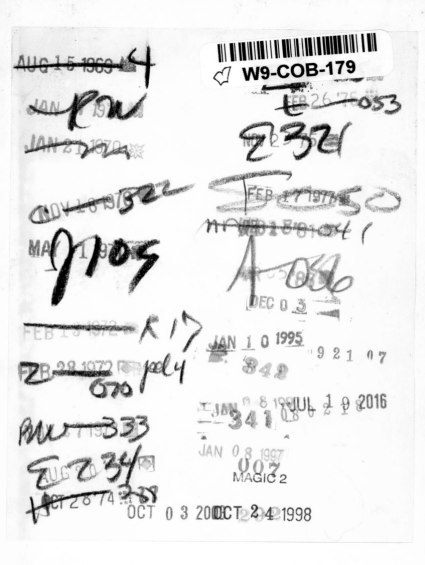

NEW DIMENSIONS IN AMERICAN HISTORY

Dedication

To Donald and Edward – whose destinies have only begun.

MANIFEST DESTINY

AND

EXPANSIONISM

IN THE

1840's

Allan O. Kownslar
Amherst Regional High School
Amherst, Massachusetts

NEW DIMENSIONS IN AMERICAN HISTORY

D. C. HEATH AND COMPANY BOSTON

CONTENTS

I

MANIFEST DESTINY

This unit is a study of the impact of an idea. That idea, prevalent in the 1840's, was the belief that a Manifest Destiny inevitably moved the United States to extend its domain across the North American continent. Focusing on the major events of the 1840's, the unit asks you to evaluate the role played during these years by the concept of a national destiny for America. Was the idea of a Manifest Destiny derived from the events of the 1840's, or was it a significant cause of those same events?

A. Ideas of National Destiny

The concept of "national destiny" is not uniquely American. As you read the following selections, which proclaim a destiny for Germany and Great Britain as well as for the United States, try to formulate a definition of national destiny. Is inevitability a dominant characteristic of the idea? Is superiority of race or superiority of institutions implicit in the idea?

1. On May 1, 1937, a year before he annexed Austria to Germany but still two years away from plunging the world into the most terrible war it has ever known, Adolf Hitler spoke to the German people:[1]

This is a Festival of the State because on this day we celebrate the regained community of the people, or rather that community

[1] Norman H. Baynes, ed., *The Speeches of Adolf Hitler, April 1922–August 1939: An English Translation of Representative Passages Arranged Under Subjects* (Oxford University Press, London and New York, 1942), 939–941.

1

of German people which has now for the first time been achieved. For to form a people is a mightier achievement than to erect a State. States come and States pass, but peoples are created for eternities. . . . The German nation has become a people.

. . . the question arises: What is it which is common to this people? Our blood? Certainly, but that community of blood has never prevented this people from shedding its best blood in civil warfare. Language? Certainly, but community of language has never prevented men who spoke one common language from failing, often for centuries, to understand one another. Is it our common economic interests? But it was precisely over economic differences that conflicts raged most fiercely. Or is it our history? That history we know: it is a tragic chronicle of per-petual wars, of disagreements between brothers. Is it a common religion? No! here too we have fought and striven with each other: for thirty years in our people's life bloodshed ever followed bloodshed and all in the name of religion. And it was not either common custom or common usage. No, it is something other than all these which guides, nay rather forces us to this community. It is, my fellow-countrymen, our common destiny, this compelling common destiny from which none can escape, our life's destiny in the world.

And it is no easy thing, it is a hard destiny, for the problems which life sets for us are harder than those of other peoples. . . . Where Nature gives everything to man in superfluity there perhaps folk need not value so highly the necessity for unity of action and of will. But we Germans have been treated by Nature in our life on this earth in a more than stepmotherly fashion. A great people, a people of endless capacity, an industrious people, a people that has the will to live, which has the courage to make demands on life, yet lives in a space which even with the greatest industry is far too small and limited to give it from its own territory the essentials for its existence. . . . Precisely because this life-struggle with us is much harder than anywhere else we are forced to draw from this fact, which is our fate, conclusions which are peculiar to our own cause. We cannot live from phrases, from platitudes and theories, but only from the results of our work, our capacity, and our intelligence. This hard life-struggle of ours is not made any easier by each going his own way, if each man says "I do what I will and what seems good to me." No, we must live one with another. No one can shut himself off from this community, because no one can escape from this common destiny. And from this hard and sober recognition of facts there arises the compelling necessity for our German community of the people. That community is the condition for the practical conduct of our life-struggle.

2. The idea of a national destiny is not new to the twentieth century. In the late nineteenth century Cecil Rhodes, a builder of the British Empire in South Africa, is reported to have said:[2]

I contend that we are the first race in the world, and that the more of the world we inhabit, the better it is for the human race. I contend that every acre added to our territory provides for the birth of more of the English race, who otherwise would not be brought into existence. Added to which the absorption of the greater portion of the world under our rule simply means the end of all wars.

3. John Ruskin, an influential contemporary of Rhodes, was a writer, art critic, and social reformer. In a notable lecture delivered at

[2] J. G. McDonald, *Rhodes: A Life* (Robert M. McBride & Company, New York, 1928), 36.

Oxford University in England he stated:[3]

. . . There is a destiny now possible to us, the highest ever set before a nation to be accepted or refused. Will you youths of England make your country again a royal throne of kings; a sceptred isle, for all the world a source of light, . . . of good will towards men? This is what England must either do or perish. She must found colonies as fast and as far as she is able, formed of her most energetic and worthiest men; seizing any piece of fruitful waste ground she can set her foot on, and there teaching her colonists that their chief virtue is to be fidelity to their country, and that their first aim is to be to advance the power of England by land and sea . . .

4. In the United States, John Louis O'Sullivan, editor of the *New York Morning News* and the *Democratic Review*, was an outspoken expansionist whose editorials popularized the idea of the Manifest Destiny of the American nation. Writing in 1845 about the proposed annexation of Texas, he said:[4]

Why, were other reasons wanting, in favor of now elevating this question of the reception of Texas into the Union, out of the lower region of our past party dissensions, up to its proper level of a high and broad nationality, it surely is to be found, found abundantly, in the manner in which other nations have undertaken to intrude themselves into it, between us and the proper parties to the case, in a spirit of hostile interference against us, for the avowed object of thwarting our policy and hampering our power, limiting our greatness and checking the fulfillment of our manifest destiny to overspread the continent allotted by Providence for the free development of our yearly multiplying millions. . . .

[3] *Ibid.*, 37.
[4] John Louis O'Sullivan, "Annexation," *Democratic Review* (1845).

5. William Gilpin, a close advisor to President James K. Polk and to Senators Thomas Hart Benton and James Buchanan, wrote the following in a report to the United States Senate, dated March 2, 1846:[5]

. . . The calm, wise man sets himself to study aright and understand clearly the deep designs of Providence — to scan the great volume of nature — to fathom, if possible, the will of the Creator, and to receive with respect what may be revealed to him.

Two centuries have rolled over our race upon this continent. From nothing we have become 20,000,000. From nothing we are grown to be in agriculture, in commerce, in civilization, and in national strength, the first among nations existing or in history. So much is our *destiny* — so far, up to this time — *transacted*, accomplished, certain, and not to be disputed. From this threshold we read the future.

The *untransacted* destiny of the American people is to subdue the continent — to rush over this vast field to the Pacific Ocean — to animate the many hundred millions of its people, and to cheer them upward — to set the principle of self-government at work — to agitate these herculean masses — to establish a new order in human affairs — to set free the enslaved — to regenerate superannuated nations — to change darkness into light — to stir up the sleep of a hundred centuries — to teach old nations a new civilization — to confirm the destiny of the human race — to carry the career of mankind to its culminating point — to cause stagnant people to be re-born — to perfect science — to emblazon history with the conquest of peace — to shed a new and resplendent glory upon mankind — to unite the world in one social family — to dissolve the spell of tyranny and exalt charity — to absolve the curse that weighs down humanity, and to shed blessings round the world!

5 William Gilpin, *Mission of the North American People, Geographical, Social, and Political*, Second Edition, Revised (J. B. Lippincott & Co., Philadelphia, 1874), 130.

6. John Gast paints Manifest Destiny in 1872.[6]

[6] *The American Heritage Book of the Pioneer Spirit* (American Heritage Company, New York, 1959), 217.

7. Selections from the Inaugural Address of President Lyndon B. Johnson, January 20, 1965.[7]

My fellow countrymen: On this occasion, the oath I have taken before you and before God, is not mine alone, but ours together. We are one nation and one people. Our fate as a nation and our future as a people rests not upon one citizen but upon all citizens.

That is the majesty and the meaning of this moment.

For every generation, there is a destiny. For some, history decides. For this generation the choice must be our own. . . .

Our destiny in the midst of change will rest on the unchanged character of our people, and on their faith.

They came here — the exile and the stranger, brave but frightened — to find a place where a man could be his own man. They made a covenant with this land. Conceived in justice, written in liberty, bound in union, it was meant one day to inspire the hopes of all mankind, and it binds us still. If we keep its terms, we shall flourish. . . .

The American covenant called on us to help show the way for the liberation of man, and that is our goal. Thus, if as a nation, there is much outside our control, as a people no stranger is outside our hope. . . .

Our nation's course is abundantly clear. We aspire to nothing that belongs to others. We seek no dominion over our fellow man, but man's dominion over tyranny and misery.

But more is required. Men want to be part of a common enterprise — a cause greater than themselves. And each of us must find a way to advance the purpose of the nation, and thus find new purpose for ourselves. Without this, we will simply become a nation of strangers. . . .

[7] *Congressional Record*, 89th Cong., 1st Sess., 985–986.

8

. . . we are a nation of believers. Underneath the clamor of building and the rush of our day's pursuits, we are believers in justice and liberty and union. And in our own Union. We believe that every man must some day be free. And we believe in ourselves. . . .

For this is what America is all about. It is the uncrossed desert and the unclimbed ridge. It is the star that is not reached and the harvest that's sleeping in the unplowed ground. . . .

But you must look within your own hearts to the old promises and to the old dreams. They will lead you best of all.

For myself, I ask only in the words of an ancient leader: "Give me now wisdom and knowledge that I may go out and come in before this people: for who can judge this thy people, that is so great?"

B. Intellectual Origins of Manifest Destiny

The concept of Manifest Destiny did not originate in the 1840's. As you examine the history of this idea, note the author and date of each selection and attempt to isolate the author's essential thought. Have their conceptions varied? How has the passage of time and events affected the ideas?

1. In September of 1867 the *Atlantic Monthly* contained an article entitled "Prophetic Voices About America: A Monograph." The following four items are drawn from that article:[8]

Sir Thomas Browne, an English physician and philosopher, wrote in 1682:

America will be the seat of the fifth empire.

George Berkeley was an Anglican bishop and a noted English philosopher. In 1726 he wrote:

> The Muse, disgusted at an age and clime
> Barren of every glorious theme,
> *In distant lands now awaits a better time,*
> Producing subjects worthy fame.
>
> *Westward the course of empire takes its way;*
> The first four acts already past,
> A fifth shall close the drama with the day;
> Time's noblest offspring is the last.

Benjamin West, an influential American painter, wrote the following in 1760:

But all things of heavenly origin, like the glorious sun, move

---

[8] "Prophetic Voices About America: A Monograph," *Atlantic Monthly* (September, 1867), 276, 278–279.

westward; and truth and art have their periods of shining and of night. Rejoice then, O venerable Rome, in thy divine destiny; for though darkness overshadow thy seats, and though thy mitred head must descend into the dust, *thy spirit immortal and undecayed already spreads towards a new world.*

In *Travels Through the Middle Settlements in North America* (1759 and 1760), a work first published in 1775, Andrew Burnaby remarked:

An idea, strange as it is visionary, has entered into the minds of the generality of mankind, *that empire is travelling westward; and every one is looking forward with eager and impatient expectation to that destined moment when America is to give the law to the rest of the world.*

2. On February 21, 1765, John Adams wrote:[9]

I always consider the settlement of America with reverence and wonder, as the opening of a grand scene and design in Providence for the illumination of the ignorant, and the emancipation of the slavish part of mankind all over the earth.

3. In "A Defence of the Constitutions of Government of the United States of America, Against the Attack of M. Turgot, in His Letter to Dr. Price, Dated the Twenty-second Day of March, 1778," Adams further declared:[10]

... Thirteen governments thus founded on the natural authority of the people alone, without a pretence of miracle or mystery, and which are destined to spread over the northern part of that whole

[9] Charles Francis Adams, *The Works of John Adams, Second President of the United States: With a Life of the Author* (Little, Brown and Company, Boston, 1856), I, 66.

[10] *Ibid.,* IV, 293.

quarter of the globe, are a great point gained in favor of the rights of mankind. The experiment is made, and has completely succeeded; it can no longer be called in question, whether authority in magistrates and obedience of citizens can be grounded on reason, morality, and the Christian religion, without the monkery of priests, or the knavery of politicians. . . .

4. In his introduction to *Common Sense* Thomas Paine wrote:[11]

The cause of America is in a great measure the cause of all mankind. Many circumstances have, and will arise, which are not local, but universal, and through which the principles of all lovers of mankind are affected, and in the event of which their affections are interested. The laying a country desolate with fire and sword, declaring war against the natural rights of all mankind, and extirpating the defenders thereof from the face of the earth, is the concern of every man to whom nature hath given the power of feeling; of which class, regardless of party censure, is

The Author

5. Letter from Richard Henry Lee, active patriot of the American Revolution, to Samuel Adams, February 4, 1775:[12]

The cause of Liberty must be under the protection of Heaven, because the Creator surely wills the happiness of his Creatures; & having joined the faculty of reasoning with our natures, he has made us capable of discerning that the true dignity and happiness of human nature are only to be found in a state of freedom. . . .

[11] Moncure Daniel Conway, ed., *The Writings of Thomas Paine* (G. P. Putnam's Sons, New York and London, 1894), I, 68.

[12] James Curtis Ballagh, ed., *The Letters of Richard Henry Lee* (The Macmillan Company, New York, 1911), 128.

6. Letter from Samuel Adams to the Reverend Samuel Cooper, a leader in prerevolutionary Boston, April 29, 1779:[13]

Nova Scotia and Canada would be a great and permanent Protection to the Fishery. But these, say some, are not Parts of the United States, and what Right should *we* have to claim them? The Cession of those Territories would prevent any Views of Britain to disturb our Peace in future and cut off a Source of corrupt British influence which issuing from them, might diffuse Mischiefe and Poison thro the States. Will not then the Possession of Nova Scotia and Canada be necessary, if we mean to make Peace upon *pacifick* Principles? If we are to have no overtures this year, and Providence blesses us with the *Spirit of Enterprize,* would it not be better for us, provided it be practicable, to wrest those Places from the Hands of the Enemy than trust to the Uncertainty of Treaty? I confess we have a Choice of Difficulties. I pray God we may surmount them all!

7. Sermon preached by Ezra Stiles, President of Yale College, on May 8, 1783:[14]

I have assumed the text only as introductory to a discourse upon the political welfare of God's American Israel, and as allusively prophetic of the future prosperity and splendor of the United States. We may, then, consider —

I. What reason we have to expect that, by the blessing of God, these states may prosper and flourish into a great American

[13] Harry Alonzo Cushing, ed., *The Writings of Samuel Adams,* IV (G. P. Putnam's Sons, New York, 1908), 149–150.

[14] John Wingate Thornton, *The Pulpit of the American Revolution: or, The Political Sermons of the Period of 1776* (Gould and Lincoln, Boston, 1860), 403, 412.

Republic, and ascend into high and distinguished honor among the nations of the earth. "To make thee high above all nations which he hath made, in praise, and in name, and in honor. . . ."

All the forms of civil polity have been tried by mankind, except one, and that seems to have been reserved in Providence to be realized in America. . . .

8. Letter from George Washington to Richard Henry Lee, December 14, 1784:[15]

To hit upon a happy medium price for the western lands, for the prevention of monopoly on one hand, and not discouraging useful settlers on the other, will, no doubt, require consideration; but should not employ too much time before it is announced. The spirit for emigration is great. People have got impatient, and, though *you cannot stop the road*, it is yet in your power to mark the way; a little while, and you will not be able to do either. . . .

9. Letter from James Madison to Marquis de Lafayette, March 20, 1785:[16]

Nature has given the use of the Mississippi to those who may settle on its waters, as she gave to the United States their independence. . . .

[15] Worthington Chauncey Ford, ed., *The Writings of George Washington, 1782–1785* (G. P. Putnam's Sons, New York and London, 1891), 429.

[16] Gaillard Hunt, ed., *The Writings of James Madison: Comprising His Public Papers and His Private Correspondence, Including Numerous Letters and Documents Now for the First Time Printed*, II (G. P. Putnam's Sons, New York and London, 1901), 121–122.

10. Letter from Thomas Jefferson to James Monroe, November 24, 1801.[17]

However our present interests may restrain us within our own limits, it is impossible not to look forward to distant times, when our rapid multiplication will expand itself beyond those limits, & cover the whole northern, if not the southern continent, with a people speaking the same language, governed in similar forms, and by similar laws. . . .

11. Speech by John Randolph in the Senate, December 16, 1811, during debates over alleged British intrusions on American rights:[18]

Sir, if you go to war it will not be for the protection of, or defence of your maritime rights. Gentlemen from the North have been taken up to some high mountain and shown all the kingdoms of the earth; and Canada seems tempting in their sight. That rich vein of Tennessee land, which is said to be even better on the other side of the lake than on this. Agrarian cupidity, not maritime right, urges the war. . . .

12. Representative John A. Harper of New Hampshire, a northern expansionist, speaking on January 4, 1812, during the House debate over the proposed acquisition of Canada:[19]

To me, sir, it appears that the Author of Nature has marked our limits in the south, by the Gulf of Mexico; and on the north, by the regions of eternal frost.

[17] Paul Leicester Ford, ed., *The Writings of Thomas Jefferson, 1801–1806* (G. P. Putnam's Sons, New York, 1897), 105.
[18] *Annals of the Congress of the United States*, 12th Cong., 1st Sess., 533.
[19] *Ibid.*, 657.

13. Note made by John Quincy Adams on November 16, 1819:[20]

Nothing that we could say or do would remove this impression until the world shall be familiarized with the idea of considering our proper dominion to be the continent of North America. From the time when we became an independent people it was as much a law of nature that this should become our pretension as that the Mississippi should flow to the sea.

14. In his *Memoirs* John Quincy Adams wrote:[21]

September 1, 1814.

I said that, wherever they [the Indians] would form settlements and cultivate lands, their possessions were undoubtedly to be respected, and always were respected, by the United States; . . . But the greater part of the Indians could never be prevailed upon to adopt this mode of life; their habits and attachments and prejudices were so averse to any settlement, that they could not reconcile themselves to any other condition than that of wandering hunters. . . . To condemn vast regions of territory to perpetual barrenness and solitude that a few hundred savages might find wild beasts to hunt upon it, was a species of game law that a nation descended from Britons would never endure. It was as incompatible with the moral as with the physical nature of things. . . . The population of the United States in 1810 passed seven millions; at this hour it undoubtedly passed eight. As it continued to increase in such proportions, was it in human experience, or in human power, to check its progress by a bond of paper purporting to exclude posterity from the natural means of subsistence which they would derive from the cultivation of the soil?

[20] Charles Francis Adams, ed., *Memoirs of John Quincy Adams*, IV (J. B. Lippincott Co., Philadelphia, 1875), 438.
[21] *Ibid.*, III, 27–28.

15. Edward Everett, Governor of Massachusetts and later United States minister to Great Britain under Tyler, on August 26, 1824, declared:[22]

Should our happy Union continue, this great continent . . . will be filled up with the highest kindred people known in history; our language will acquire an extension which no other ever possessed; and the empire of the mind, with nothing to resist its sway, will attain an expansion . . . we can but partly conceive. The vision is too magnificent to be fully borne; — a mass of two or three hundred millions, not chained to the oar, like the same number in China, by a stupefying despotism, but held in their several orbits of nation and state, by the grand representative attraction; bringing to bear, on every point, the concentrated energy of such a host; calling into competition so many minds; uniting into one great national feeling the hearts of so many freemen, all to be guided, moved, and swayed, by the master spirits of the time!

[Five years later, on June 29, 1829, Governor Everett stated:]

. . . the growth of your western country is not merely the progress of its citizens in numerical multiplication. It is civilization personified and embodied, going forth to take possession of the land. It is the *principle* of our institutions, advancing not so much with the toilsome movement of human agency, but rather like the grand operations of sovereign *Providence.* It seems urged along its stupendous course, as the earth itself is propelled in orbit, silent and calm, like the moving planet, with a speed we cannot measure; yet not, like that, without a monument to mark its way through the vacant regions of space, but scattering ham-

[22] Edward Everett, *Orations and Speeches on Various Occasions*, 2nd Edition, I (Charles C. Little and James Brown, Boston, 1850), 33–34, 210.

lets, and villages, and cities on its path, — the abodes of civilized and prosperous millions.

16. Representative James Moore Wayne, a Jacksonian Democrat from Georgia, speaking May 24, 1830, in the House on the question of Indian removal:[23]

Vattel [noted authority on international law] says, folio 92, section 81: "The whole earth is appointed for the nourishment of the inhabitants; but it would be incapable of doing so, was it uncultivated. Every nation is, then, obliged, by the law of nature, to cultivate the ground that has fallen to its share; and it has no right to expect or require assistance from others any further than as the land in its possession is incapable of furnishing it with necessaries. . . ."

What though the Indian roved through the forests of America contemporaneously with the wanderings of God's chosen people in their escape from Egyptian bondage — time could give to him no right to more of the soil than he could cultivate; and the decree which denied him to be lord of the domain, was the Almighty's command to his creatures to till the earth.

17. In summary, Samuel Flagg Bemis, noted historian, commented:[24]

For a fortunate century after the overthrow of Napoleon mankind escaped another world war. After 1823 American diplomacy could no longer reap such advantages from the distresses of Europe as before. Thanks to a half-century of conflict, the first republic of the New World, and the other republics following it, had rooted themselves too sturdily in the international soil to be weeded out by the monarchies of Europe. The remaining years

[23] *Register of Debates in Congress,* 21st Cong., 1st Sess., 1125.

[24] Samuel Flagg Bemis, *A Diplomatic History of the United States* (Henry Holt and Company, New York, 1950), 215–216.

of the nineteenth century were to witness throughout the vacant western reaches of this continent a process of self-sustained expansion destined to make the United States a world power fronting on the two great oceans of civilization and ready to control an artificial waterway between them. It was a period of consciously aggressive expansion interrupted by the growing-pains and international risks of the Civil War, and even disguised by decades of digestive tranquillity in the 'seventies and 'eighties, to end in a spectacular climax of expansive force in 1898. Expansion expressed the pent-up forces of the developing national spirit in the United States. It has remained its principal and most successful manifestation. It is embodied in the phrase Manifest Destiny, first coined in 1845, but invoked in spirit, in word and deed, by American statesmen from Jefferson and John Quincy Adams to Seward and Charles Sumner, not to mention the expansionists of 1898, the Mahans, the Lodges and the Roosevelts. Manifest Destiny represented a widespread and swelling popular conviction that it was indeed the manifest destiny of the Republic to expand by peaceful process and by the force of republican example and principles of government over the whole of the continent of North America. It was not based on militarism. Throughout the history of the expansionist movement the United States (except for the interlude of the Civil War) remained a nation with the smallest of armies, without conscription, with a minimum of naval force. Unsympathetically philosophers have analyzed the essential self-interest of Manifest Destiny, under its cloak of pious phrases; but we must remember that American expansion across a practically empty continent despoiled no nation unjustly, and that there is no American today who would want to see that expansion undone. Manifest Destiny might much better be described as Manifest Opportunity.

II

ISSUES, ACTIONS, AND THE
ELECTION OF 1844

An examination of relationships is complex and demanding. This
section contains a number of items which relate to the question of
destiny. To determine the nature of those relationships is the principal
focus of this section.

A. Pre-Election Issues, Interests, and Territorial Claims in Texas

American interests in Texas were of historic and practical origin.
When the United States purchased Louisiana from France in 1803, it
also obtained a title to Texas. With the Adams-Onís Agreement of
1819 the United States ceded that title to Spain and in return received
Florida.

In the same year as the Adams-Onís Agreement, Moses Austin, a
native of Durham, Connecticut, applied for and received a grant of
land with permission from Spanish authorities to settle a colony in
Texas. Austin died shortly thereafter and his son, Stephen, under a
newly created Mexican government independent of Spain, established a colony between the Brazos and Colorado rivers.

With problems of organizing a new government becoming greater
and because of independent actions by Texan-Americans, Mexico
centralized its government under the influence of Santa Anna, general

of the army. On March 2, 1836, the Texans declared themselves independent and established the Lone Star Republic. Sam Houston, an old friend of Andrew Jackson, became commander-in-chief of the Texas army.

In February of 1836 Santa Anna marched his army of 5000 men to San Antonio. There for twelve days he besieged the Alamo, a mission held by Texans under the leadership of Colonel William B. Travis. Fighting with Travis were such legendary heroes as Davy Crockett and James Bowie. After numerous charges by Santa Anna's forces the Mexicans finally overran the Alamo and all 183 men defending it died. Yet the defeat proved costly for the Mexicans. Time spent attacking the Alamo gave Sam Houston time to organize his forces and later defeat the Mexicans at San Jacinto on April 22, 1836.

With independence gained but not diplomatically recognized by Mexico, the Texans sought annexation to the United States. The United States government, however, took no action. Fearing a prolonged delay by the United States on annexation, Texas pondered an alliance with Great Britain which would persuade Mexico to recognize the Lone Star Republic's independence. Many American slaveholders became alarmed over the possibility that Texas, as a means of returning England's favor, would abolish slavery. Still other Americans feared a Texas-England alliance that possibly could lead to European influence in the Southwest.

This section deals with the causes of the Texas Revolution as well as American interests and claims to Texas. Note particularly the main interests of immigrants to Texas.

1. In discussing the causes of the Texas revolt against Mexico in 1836, William C. Binkley, a historian of that conflict, wrote:[1]

---

[1] William C. Binkley, *The Texas Revolution* (Louisiana State University Press, Baton Rouge, 1952), 5–6, 33–34.

Three problems which had already caused the colonists some concern were the requirement that all settlers in Texas must be Catholics, the recurring indications of Mexican opposition to slavery, and the failure to make adequate provision for the machinery of local government through which they might have a direct voice in the administering of their own affairs and the maintaining of order. Thus far, however, the authorities had shown little disposition to raise any question concerning the religious affiliations of the immigrants; and on the question of slavery, prohibitory measures which had been adopted by both the state and the national governments were virtually nullified when Mexican officials collaborated with the colonists in working out a system of contract labor which permitted its continuation in fact if not in name. But in both cases the continued existence of the restrictions constituted a potential danger that could not be ignored. The third problem, on the other hand, grew out of a need for positive action. In their efforts to obtain a more adequate system of local administration the Anglo-Americans were simply following the precedents of earlier frontier experience in the United States, but the suspicious Mexican mind construed their request as evidence of a plot to undermine Mexican institutions, instigated no doubt by the aggressive neighbor to the north. The response was the passage of the famous law of April 6, 1830, which placed a ban on further immigration into Texas from the United States and provided for the garrisoning of the province with convict soldiers to ensure the enforcement of Mexican laws....

As if these fundamental questions of securing satisfactory arrangements in their general political, economic, and social conditions were not enough to keep the Texans fully occupied, certain special difficulties were gradually demanding more and more attention. For example, the facilities for adequate communication between the different parts of the province had not kept pace with increasing needs, and the Anglo-Americans were trying with little success to interest the state government in the development of a program of internal improvements which would provide good roads and improve the usability of the numerous streams. They were also concerned over the present danger of depredations from the Indian tribes along their frontier, but the only response that came to their requests for permission to organize their own militia force was a suggestion from the government that convict troops would be sent to handle the problem. More serious than either of these, however, was the adoption by the state legislature of 1834 of a new series of land laws by which the *empresario* system was abolished and the gates apparently opened to speculation on a wholesale plan. To the Texans this seemed to mean the concentration of land in the hands of a few at the expense of the people in general, and from their point of view the whole episode furnished a clearer illustration of the defectiveness of the state government.

2. In 1836 Senator Thomas Hart Benton, an ardent expansionist, defended the Texans in their rebellion against Mexico:[2]

Great is the mistake which has prevailed in Mexico, and in some parts of the United States, on the character of the population which has gone to Texas. It has been common to disparage and to stigmatize them. Nothing could be more unjust; and, speaking from knowledge, either personally or well acquired, . . . I can vindicate them from erroneous imputations, and place their conduct and character on the honorable ground which they deserve to occupy. . . . They have gone, not as intruders, but as grantees;

[2] Thomas Hart Benton, *Thirty Years' View or, A History of the Working of the American Government for Thirty Years, from 1820 to 1850* (D. Appleton and Company, New York, 1854), I, 674, 675.

and to become a barrier between the Mexicans and the marauding Indians who infested their borders. . . .

Just in its origin, valiant and humane in its conduct, sacred in its object, the Texian revolt has illustrated the Anglo-Saxon character, and given it new titles to the respect and admiration of the world.

It shows that liberty, justice, valor — moral, physical, and intellectual power — discriminate that race wherever it goes. Let our America rejoice, let Old England rejoice, that the Brassos and Colorado, new and strange names — streams far beyond the western bank of the Father of Floods — have felt the impress, and witnessed the exploits of a people sprung from their loins, and carrying their language, laws, and customs, their *magna charta* and its glorious privileges, into new regions and far distant climes. . . .

3. John Holland Jenkins recalled of his early days in Texas:[3]

About the mddle of October in the year 1828 my father left his old home in Alabama and came west, intending to grow up with the new country — at least in a financial point of view. . . .

Constantly in the fall and summer of 1829 [1830] we would have additions to our small band of settlers — men, old and young, from all parts of the United States, coming to try, or look at, Texas. These newcomers were very welcome, for we were not only glad to get news direct from the great world of commerce now so remote from us, but we were also glad to be strengthened in numbers, in view of probable assault by the roving bands of savages, whose visits were constantly growing more frequent and more aggressive. . . .

3 John Holland Jenkins, III, ed., *Recollections of Early Texas: The Memoirs of John Holland Jenkins* (University of Texas Press, Austin, 1958), 3, 12, 17–18, 19.

A half-covered log cabin with a dirt floor had already been prepared for us by my father, and very near we had the luxury of a fine spring. Building cowpen, lot, and such things first busied the men, then the small stock of cattle we brought on from our first home on Barton's Creek.

Ah! What a country was West Texas then. It almost "flowed with milk and honey," and in truth nothing could be more beautiful than the broad plains covered with wild rye and the finest grass the world ever afforded. Feasting upon such luxuries the faithful old cows gave an abundance of milk the whole year round, and now when summer's drought or winter's blight comes upon us, and our stock suffer so much, despite every effort we make, it is no wonder that we wish for *the good old days*, when the land stood "dressed in living green. . . ."

. . . until 1833 our new lives were comparatively quiet, so that we were gradually growing accustomed to the realities of the "western wilds." The simplicity and limit of our farming operations in those days would at least be suggestive of rest and peace to the poor farmers of the present [1884] who are trying so hard to make money under the rule of *King Cotton*. Our farms were comprised of about ten acres in all, most of which was planted to corn, with just a little cotton, only about ten or twelve rows!

4. David B. Edward, the Preceptor of Gonzales Seminary in Texas, included in his emigrants' guide to Texas in 1836:[4]

There are no poor people here, if land makes rich; and none rich, if money is wealth. The poor and the rich, to use the correlatives where distinction there is none, get the same quantity

[4] David B. Edward, *The History of Texas: or, The Emigrants', Farmer's, and Politician's Guide to the Character, Climate, Soil and Productions of That Country* (J. A. James & Co., Cincinnati, 1836), 278.

of land on arrival; and if they do not continue equal, it is for want of good management on the one part, or superior industry and sagacity on the other. By the land which they receive, all can be busy and happy. . . . Industrious farmers certainly do well in Texas and cannot fail of success, if abundant crops and a ready market with high prices will satisfy them. Substantial planters, with capital and hands, may enlarge their operations to any extent, and with enormous profits.

5. Commenting on immigration to Texas, *The Northern Standard* of October 30, 1844, stated:[5]

Two gentlemen from Missouri, who have just arrived, for the purpose of selecting a location to move to, state that they counted all the emigrant wagons as they passed between Fayetteville, Arkansas, and Doaksville, some coming, and some returning from the Trinity country. There were 225 wagons coming, and 75 returning. As they met on the road, the faint hearted, who were going back, would tell their difficulties, which were all embraced in the want of provisions, arising from the want of means to get them, with the addition that those who turn back from a good work always make, namely, that every body that started with them was doing, or about to do likewise — which was untrue. But they stopped none — they deterred none. Those whose faces were turned hitherward, kept on; and being warned of the high price of corn on Trinity, will generally wait till spring, before they go there, spending the winter where corn is cheaper and easier obtained. Even now, as we write, four wagons are passing the office from Green county, Illinois, with "Polk Dallas, Oregon and Texas," painted on the covers. These intend to direct to the forks of the Trinity.

5 *Niles' National Register*, December 28, 1844, 257.

6. Speaking in the Senate on February 22, 1845, on the subject of claims to Texas, Senator Chester Ashley of Arkansas argued:[6]

Mr. Jefferson, in his letter to Mr. Bowdoin, 11th July, 1806, Jeff. cor. p. 59, says:

"With respect to your western boundary, your instructions will be your guide. I will only add as a comment to them, that we are attached to the retaining the bay of St. Bernard, because it was the first establishment of the unfortunate La Salle, *was the cradle of Louisiana*, and more incontestable covered and conveyed to us by France under that name, than any other spot in the country."

"St. Bernard's Bay, bay in the gulf of Mexico on the coast of Texas. Lou. 96, 50, w.; lat. 29, 30, n. — *Worcester's Gazetteer,* ed. 1823."

Louisiana was ceded by France to Spain in 1761, and was retroceded by Spain to France in 1800, and occupied by France. By the treaty of Paris of the 30th April, 1803, it was ceded by France to the United States, and the possession delivered by the French authorities in 1804.

Mr. Madison, expressing his own views, and those of Mr. Jefferson, in a letter of the 31st March, 1804 says that Louisiana "extended westwardly to Rio Bravo, otherwise called Rio Bravo Del Norte. *Orders* were accordingly obtained from the Spanish authorities for the delivery of *all the posts* on the west side of the Mississippi:" and in a letter of the 31st January, 1804, Mr. Madison states that M. Laussat, the commissioner by whom the French government *delivered the possession of Louisiana to us,* announced *"the Del Norte as its true boundary."* In a letter of the 8th July, 1804, Mr. Madison declares the opposition of Mr. Jefferson to the *"relinquishment of any territory whatever eastward of the Bravo."*

[6] *Congressional Globe*, 28th Cong., 2nd Sess., Appendix, 284.

Mr. Monroe, in a letter of the 8th November, 1803, *encloses documents* which, he says, *"prove incontestably"* that the boundary of Louisiana is "the Rio Bravo to the west;" and Mr. Pinckney unites with Mr. Monroe in a similar declaration; and on the 20th April, 1805, in a letter to Mr. Madison, they assert our title to be unquestionable. Mr. Monroe, in his letters of January 19 and June 10, 1816, says that none could question *"our title to Texas,"* and concurs with Mr. Jefferson and Mr. Madison in the opinion *"that our title to the Del Norte was as clear as to the island of New Orleans."*

Mr. John Quincy Adams, in a letter to Don Onís of the 12th March, 1818, says:

"The claims of France always did extend westward to the Rio Bravo," * * * "She *always* claimed the territory which you call Texas, as being within the limits and forming a part of Louisiana."

And he further says:

"Well might Messrs. Pinckney and Monroe write to M. Cervallos, in 1805, that the claim of the United States to the boundary of the Rio Bravo was as clear as their right to the island of New Orleans."

And in his letter of the 31st of October, 1818, he says:

"Our title to Texas is established beyond the power of further controversy."

Mr. Adams, in his letter of instructions to Mr. George Graham of June 2, 1818, says:

"The President wishes you to proceed with all convenient speed to that place (Galveston) unless, as is not improbable you should in the progress of the journey, learn that they have abandoned or been driven from it. Should they have removed to Matagorda, *or any other place north of the Rio Bravo and within the territory claimed by the United States,* you will repair thither, without, however, exposing yourself to be captured by any

Spanish military force. When arrived you will, in a suitable manner, make known to the chief or leader of the expedition your authority from the government of the United States, and express the surprise with which the President has seen possession thus taken without authority from the United States, of a *place within their territorial limits, and upon which no lawful settlement can be made without their sanction.* You will call upon him explicitly to avow under what national authority they profess to act and take care that due warning be given to the whole body that *the place is within the United States, who will suffer no permanent settlement to be made there, under any authority other than their own."*

Mr. Clay, in his speech on the Spanish treaty, April 3, 1820 (Mallory, vol. 1, pp. 400 and 401,) said:

"The title to the Perdido on the one side, and to the Rio del Norte on the other, rested on the same principle — the priority of discovery, and of occupation by France; the principle observed among European nations having contiguous settlements being that the unoccupied space between them about be equally divided. In 1685, he (La Salle) made an establishment on the Bay of St. Bernard, west of the Colorado, emptying into it. The nearest Spanish settlement was Panuco; and the Rio del Norte, about the midway line, became the common boundary."

Mr. Clay also, in his letter of the 17th April, 1844, published in the *National Intelligencer,* says:

"The United States acquired a title to Texas, extending, as I believe, to the Rio del Norte, by the treaty of Louisiana. They ceded and relinquished that title to Spain by the treaty of 1819, by which the Sabine was substituted for the Rio del Norte as our western boundary."

But he would not enlarge nor add to the small portion of existing evidence that he had referred to. It could readily be shown by the concurrent authority of every prominent public man in the country — by the public ministers of the United States, France, and Spain, and by the whole history of the times, that the true boundaries of Louisiana extended to the Rio del Norte, (or the Rio Bravo, as it is sometimes called,) and that therefore, by the treaty of 1803, we did acquire all of Texas, including lands and *inhabitants.*

B. Pre-Election Issues, Interests, and Territorial Claims in Oregon

During the 1840's Americans also became more interested in historic claims to Oregon. Since the early 1800's conflicts over Oregon had diminished. In 1818 the United States and Great Britain signed a treaty which provided for a joint occupation of the territory. Both parties, upon a year's notice, could terminate the agreement. Through the Adams-Onís Treaty of 1819, Spain gave up its claim north of 42°. Russia relinquished its title after announcement of the Monroe Doctrine in 1823.

Most active in early settlement were the fur trading interests. In 1811 John Jacob Astor had established a fur-trading company in Oregon. Yet fourteen years later the English-owned Hudson Bay Company at Fort Vancouver controlled the fur industry in Oregon. By the 1830's, however, the nature of the pioneers changed as men like Marcus Whitman, the Presbyterian minister, began to migrate. By the first part of the next decade American immigration to that country had greatly increased. Prompted by the Panic of 1837 and the hard times that followed, many Americans caught "Oregon Fever" and, with the opening of the Oregon Trail in 1843, began to migrate to places such as the Willamette valley. By 1846 Americans out-numbered the British in Oregon six to one.

As you read this section, note particularly American interests and claims to Oregon.

1. Referring to "Oregon Fever," *The Expositor* of Independence, Missouri, said on May 3, 1845:[7]

... Even while we write, we see a long train of wagons coming through our busy streets; they are hailed with shouts of welcome by their fellow voyagers, and, to judge from the pleased expression on every face, it "all goes merry as a marriage bell." On looking out at the passing train, we see among the foremost a very comfortably covered wagon, one of the sheets drawn aside, and an extremely nice looking lady seated inside very quietly sewing; the bottom of the wagon is carpeted; there are two or three chairs, and at one end there is a bureau, surmounted by a mirror; various articles of ornament and convenience hang around the sides – a perfect prairie boudoir. Blessed be woman! Shedding light and happiness where'er she goes; with her the wild prairie will be a paradise! Blessed be him who gave us this connecting link be-tween heaven and man to win us from our wilder ways. Hold on there; this is getting entirely too sentimental; but we don't care who laughs, we felt better and happier when we looked on this picture than we may express ... and now comes team after team, each drawn by six or eight stout oxen, and such drivers! positively sons of Anals! not one of them less than six feet two in his stock-ings. Whoo ha! Go it boys! We're in a perfect *Oregon fever*.

2. Hall J. Kelley did much to publicize the advantages of living in

[7] *Niles' Weekly Register*, LXVIII, May 31, 1845, 203.

the West. In the *American Traveller,* September 25, 1832, Kelley defined the benefits accorded both to the individual and to the country from the settlement of Oregon:[8]

Each man and each youth, over 14 years of age, will receive 200 acres of land. Each unmarried female, over 14 years, will likewise receive 200 acres. Every individual above that age, will be required to pay $50, for which sum he will be carried to Oregon, and receive a right to 200 acres of land. Children will pay a less sum, and receive no land. Emigrants will furnish their own bedding and small stores. Other freight will be taken in vessels round Cape Horn, at $2 a barrel. Farmers and mechanics will carry their tools, and such materials as they may immediately want. As small a quantity of baggage as possible must be carried by the overland expedition.

* * * * * *

Of the advantages of settling the Oregon country, Hall J. Kelley wrote:

First. The occupancy of it, by three thousand of the active sons of America freedom, would secure it from the possession of another nation, and from augmenting the power and physical resources of an enemy. It might save that and this country from the disastrous consequences of a foreign and corrupt population; and benefit mankind by a race of people, whose past lives, affording the most honourable testimony of their character, would be a pledge for their future conduct, and a full indemnity for all expenses incurred in their behalf.

3. Francis Parkman, historian and witness to much of the westward

[8] Archer Butler Hulbert, ed., *The Call of the Columbia: Iron Men and Saints Take the Oregon Trail* (The Stewart Commission of Colorado College and the Denver Public Library, Denver, 1934), 59–60, 63.

expansion of the 1840's, wrote in his American classic, *The Oregon Trail*:[9]

Last Spring, 1846, was a busy season in the city of St. Louis. Not only were emigrants from every part of the country preparing for the journey to Oregon and California, but an unusual number of traders were making ready their wagons and outfits for Santa Fe. The hotels were crowded, and the gunsmiths and saddlers were kept constantly at work in providing arms and equipments for the different parties of travelers. Steamboats were leaving the levee and passing up the Missouri, crowded with passengers on their way to the frontier.

* * * * * *

The passengers on board the "Radnor" corresponded with her freight. In her cabin were Sante Fe traders, gamblers, speculators, and adventurers of various descriptions, and her steerage was crowded wth Oregon emigrants, "mountain men," negroes, and a party of Kansas Indians, who had been on a visit to St. Louis.

* * * * * *

In five or six days we began to see signs of the great western movement that was taking place. Parties of emigrants, with their tents and wagons, were encamped on open spots near the bank, on their way to the common rendezvous at Independence. On a rainy day, near sunset, we reached the landing of this place, which is some miles from the river, on the extreme frontier of Missouri. The scene was characteristic, for here were represented at one view the most remarkable features of this wild and enterprising region. On the muddy shore stood some thirty or forty dark

[9] Francis Parkman, *The Oregon Trail: Sketches of Prairie and Rocky-Mountain Life*, Eighth Edition (Little, Brown and Company, Boston, 1883), 1, 2, 3, 5–6.

slavish-looking Spaniards, gazing stupidly at one of the Sante Fe companies, whose wagons were crowded together on the banks above. In the midst of these, crouching over a smouldering fire, was a group of Indians, belonging to a remote Mexican tribe. One or two French hunters from the mountains, with their long hair and buckskin dresses, were looking at the boat; and seated on a log close at hand were three men, with rifles lying across their knees. The foremost of these, a tall, strong figure, with a clear blue eye and an open, intelligent face, might very well represent that race of restless and intrepid pioneers whose axes and rifles have opened a path from the Alleghanies to the western prairies. He was on his way to Oregon, probably a more congenial field to him than any that now remained on this side of the great plains.

❈ ❈ ❈ ❈ ❈ ❈

. . . The emigrants, for whom our friends professed such contempt, were encamped on the prairie about eight or ten miles distant, to the number of a thousand or more, and new parties were constantly passing out from Independence to join them. They were in great confusion, holding meetings, passing resolutions, and drawing up regulations, but unable to unite in the choice of leaders to conduct them across the prairie. Being at leisure one day, I rode over to Independence. The town was crowded. A multitude of shops had sprung up to furnish the emigrants and Santa Fe traders with necessaries for their journey; and there was an incessant hammering and banging from a dozen blacksmiths' sheds, where the heavy wagons were being repaired, and the horses and oxen shod. The streets were thronged with men, horses, and mules. While I was in the town, a train of emigrant wagons from Illinois passed through, to join the camp on the prairie, and stopped in the principal street. A multitude of healthy

34

children's faces were peeping out from under the covers of the wagons. Here and there a buxom damsel was seated on horseback holding over her sunburnt face an old umbrella or a parasol, once gaudy enough, but now miserably faded. The men, very sober looking countrymen, stood about their oxen; and as I passed noticed three old fellows, who, with their long whips in their hands, were zealously discussing the doctrine of regeneration. The emigrants, however, are not all of this stamp. Among them are some of the vilest outcasts in the country. I have often perplexed myself to divine the various motives that give impulse to this migration; but whatever they may be, whether an insane hope of a better condition in life, or a desire of shaking off restraints of law and society, or mere restlessness, certain it is, that multitudes bitterly repent the journey, and, after they have reached the land of promise, are happy enough to escape from it.

4. Letter from Marcus Whitman, one of the first missionaries to Oregon, to the Rev. L. P. Judson, dated November 5, 1846 Waiilatpu.[10]

. . . Within the same time I have returned to my field of labour & in my return brought a large Immigration of about one thousand individuals safely through the long & the last part of it an untried rout to the western shores of the Continent. Now that they were once safely conducted through; three successive Immigration have followed after them & two routs for wagons are now open into the Wallamette [Willamette] valley. Mark; had I been of your mind I should have slept & now the Jesuit Papists would have been in quiet possession of this the only spot in the western hor

[10] Archer Butler Hulbert and Dorothy Printup Hulbert, eds., *Marcus Whitman, Crusader, Part Three, 1843 to 1847* (The Stewart Commission of Colorado College and the Denver Public Library, Denver, 1941), 199–200

son [horizon] of America not before their own. They were fast fixing themselves here, & had we Missionaries had no American population to come in to hold on & give stability it would have been but a smal[l] work for them & the friends of English interests which they had also ful[l]y avowed to have routed us & then the Country might have slept in their hands forever. . . .

This is a country requiring devoted pious labourers in the service of our Lord. There are many & great advantages offered to those who come at once (soon). A mile square or 640 acres of land such as you may select & that of the best of land and in a near proximity to a vast Ocean & in a mild climate where stock feed out all winter is not a small boon. Nor should men of piety & principle leave it all to be taken by . . . worldly men.

5. A contemporaneous description of Oregon in the 1840's:[11]

At present the most fruitful source of supply for settlers in Oregon, is the United States of America. Emigrations have arrived in the country, direct from Missouri, every fall, since 1839. In 1840 and 1841, the parties were comparatively small, but in 1842 the emigration numbered one hundred and eleven persons in all. In 1843 it increased to eight hundred persons, who emigrated principally in ox-wagons, and drove before them fifteen hundred head of meat cattle. In 1844, the number was about the same as the preceding year. In 1845, it increased to nearly three thousand souls, with some two or three thousand head of cattle.

These emigrations, for the most part, are composed of persons from the Western States, but in them might be found persons from almost every State in the Union, even the most Eastern, Maine herself had supplied several.

[11] Rev. Gustavus Hines, *Oregon: Its History, Condition, and Prospects* . . . (Geo. H. Derby and Co., Buffalo, 1851), 415–416.

Many of these adventurers are of that class of persons who have always hovered on the frontiers of civilization, and have been pushing on in search of a "better country, not an heavenly," until they have passed the utmost borders of civilized society. Penetrating entirely through the deep recesses of savage life, they have finally emerged from the deep defiles of the Cascade Mountains, into the lovely valleys of Oregon, where they have found, at least in embryo, the blessings of Christianity and civilization; and here most of them, some from choice, and others from the impossibility of getting away, come to the conclusion to erect their tabernacles for life. The enterprise of these parties has far outstripped the most sanguine expectations of the English writer in a London paper, who a few years ago, remarked, that, "Even the persevering Yankees would not think of emigrating to Oregon in their ox-wagons." If this writer had possessed the eye of omniscience, he would have seen, at the very time he was penning it, a score of Yankee wagons, drawn by sixty yoke of oxen, winding their way through the deep passes of the Rocky Mountains, bound for the Oregon.

5. Speaking in the Senate on March 12, 1846, David Rice Atchison, Whig from Missouri, stated:[12]

Speeches and reports made in Congress from 1840 to '43 had been diligently distributed throughout the West by western Senators; and the Representatives in the other House had called the attention of the people of the West to the condition and advantages of this new territory. The first emigrants who ever went into that country for purposes of settlement and agriculture went from the western frontiers of the State of Missouri — and what had been

---

[12] *Congressional Globe,* 29th Cong., 1st Sess., Appendix, 349.

their inducement? Mr. A. knew them well; he was personally acquainted with the men who went; and he knew that what they expected had been that this Government would extend over them the laws of the United States, that it would make to them donations in land, and would see that they were protected in their rights and property. They had been taught to believe that it was an object with this Government to take possession of that territory, and they were just the men to do it. It had been said that they were actuated merely by a wild spirit of adventure; and that perhaps might have had its influence with some; but it was not this alone which carried them to Oregon. Wild as that spirit might be, it never could have induced them to encounter such dangers and difficulties as lay between their homes and this new country. Most of them went there to better their condition. Many of them were poor men with large families. They expected ample grants of land, and they were willing to risk their lives and encounter every privation and hardship that they might better their own condition, provide a home for their children, and carry out the policy of the Government. . . .

7. Speech by Senator George Evans, Whig from Maine, March 9 and 10, 1846.[13]

We derive our title to the country on the northwest coast of America, which gentlemen of late have chosen to call "Oregon," from three distinct sources. First, from discovery: the discovery of the Columbia river, from the sea, by Captain Gray, in 1792; and, from its head-water, by Lewis and Clarke, in 1804 and 1805. Secondly, from the cession of Louisiana by France in 1803. On the ground of discovery, we can claim no more than the river Columbia, and the country drained by it and its branches. This

[13] *Congressional Globe,* 29th Cong., 1st Sess., Appendix, 573.

does not carry us beyond the forty-ninth parallel, if so far. By the cession of Louisiana, we gain nothing beyond that same parallel – not an inch. The third source of our title, and that which covers all the others, and which is said not to be inconsistent with them, is the cession by Spain in the Florida treaty. That conveys the whole, provided Spain had the whole to convey.

8. Thomas Hart Benton of Missouri spoke in the Senate on June 3, 1844:[14]

After twenty-five years, the American population has begun to extend itself to the Oregon. Some hundreds went a few years ago; a thousand went last year; two thousand are now setting out from the frontiers of Missouri; tens of thousands are meditating the adventure. I say to them all, Go on! the Government will follow you, and will give you protection and land. . . . let the emigrants rely upon it. It is the genius of our people to go ahead, and it is the practice of our Government to follow, and eventually to protect and reward the bold pioneers who open the way to new countries, and subdue the wilderness for their country. They will get protection, both civil, military, and naval; for a Government will be established for them, and ships of war will visit their coast, and enter their river. Lands will be granted to them; land to the father and to the mother; land to the young men and the young women over eighteen; land to all the children. . . .

Let the emigrants go on, and carry their rifles: We want thirty thousand rifles in the valley of the Oregon; they will make all quiet there, in the event of a war with Great Britain for the dominion of that country. The war, if it comes, will not be topical; it will not be confined to Oregon; but will embrace the possession

[14] Thomas Hart Benton, *Abridgment of the Debates of Congress, From 1789 to 1856*, XV (D. Appleton and Company, New York, 1861), 141, 142.

of the two powers throughout the globe. Thirty thousand rifles on the Oregon will annihilate the Hudson Bay Company, drive them off our continent, quiet their Indians, and protect the American interests in the remote regions of the upper Missouri, the Platte, and the Arkansas, and in all the vast region of the Rocky Mountains.

Besides the recovery of the country lost, or jeopardized by our diplomacy of 1818, the settlers in Oregon will also recover and open for us *the North American road to India!* This road lies through the South Pass, and the mouth of the Oregon; and as soon as the settlements are made, our portion of the North American continent will immediately commence its Asiatic trade on this new and national route. This great question I explored some years ago, and only refer to it now to give a glimpse of the brilliant destiny which awaits the population of the Oregon valley.

9. The *New-England Magazine* of February, 1832, contained an article by William Joseph Snelling which was critical of those advocating westward migration. (See, for example, Reading 2 by Hall J. Kelley):[15]

We can see no advantage in Oregon which the emigrant may not secure in the state of Maine. The sea washes the shores of both. The soil is good in both. There are fisheries pertaining to both. If the climate of Oregon is milder, it is not proved that it is better. There is waste land in both. There is plenty of timber in both. Maine has these advantages. Her inhabitants are under the protection of the laws. They are numerous enough to protect each other. They have free communication with every part of the world. There is no art or science of which she does not possess at least the rudiments. All that can be done in Oregon, within a

[15] Archer Butler Hulbert, ed., *The Call of the Columbia: Iron Men and Saints Take the Oregon Trail* (The Stewart Commission of Colorado College and the Denver Public Library, Denver, 1934), 88–89.

hundred years [1932], is already done in Maine. Above all, she has no Indians to root out with fire and sword, fraudulent treaties, or oppressive enactments.

That a party of young, brave, hardy men may cross the continent to the mouth of the Columbia, we know; but that a large body of the inhabitants of New England, wholly unacquainted with Indian life, and encumbered with baggage and their families, can do so, we hold impossible. We think we have proved that it is so. Our facts cannot be disputed, and the inference is as clear as a geometrical demonstration. We do not know that the prime mover of the folly we have exposed is actuated by any evil motive; we do not believe it. We look upon him as an unfortunate man, who, deluded himself, is deluding others, and conceive it our duty to warn those who are about to follow him on the road to ruin. To conclude, we advise those who have been so unfortunate as to embark on this enterprise to erase their names from the list as soon as possible. If they cannot retrieve the money they may have advanced, let them consider it better lost, than followed to Oregon, and be thankful that they have so escaped.

C. The Election of 1844

By the time for the election of 1844 the country was excited about what to do not only with Texas but with Oregon as well. Texas became an important issue when President John Tyler had Abel Upshur, Secretary of State, advise Isaac Van Zandt, the Texan representative, that the United States might favorably view annexation of the Lone Star Republic. Problems arose when Upshur's successor, John C. Calhoun, by introducing the slavery question, intensified northern and abolitionist opposition to a treaty with Texas. The Senate on June 8, 1844, rejected annexation by a decisive vote.

Only a month before, the Whigs had met in Baltimore and nominated Henry Clay for President. Clay opposed the annexation of Texas. The Democrats assembled for their convention in June. Martin Van Buren, party leader since the 1830's and a former President, was the Democrats' likely choice. However, as an antiexpansionist he failed to obtain the required two-thirds approval of the delegates. A stalemate developed until James K. Polk of Tennessee emerged as a "dark horse" candidate, and from the struggle Polk emerged as the nominee.

As you read about this election, note the role of the idea of a Manifest Destiny as it appeared to have operated on the political situation.

1. As reported by a contemporary, Senator Stephen A. Douglas viewed the political situation in 1844 as follows:[16]

The Texas question, thus sprung upon the country by Mr. Tyler's administration, was the controlling element in the Presidential election of 1844. The Whig party assembled in convention at Baltimore early in May of that year, and nominated Henry Clay as their candidate for President. The delegates had already been elected by the conventions in the several States to the Democratic National Convention at Baltimore, in June, 1844, a large majority, and in fact nearly all of them, pledged and instructed to vote for the nomination of Mr. Van Buren, as the Democratic candidate. Mr. Clay and Mr. Van Buren had, for months previous to the assembling of either convention, been universally regarded as the chosen candidates of their respective parties, and no other candidates had been thought of by either party, until Mr. Tyler threw this Texas fire-brand or bomb-shell into their midst. Mr. Clay and Mr. Van Buren each was confident that he could beat the other, on

16 J. Madison Cutts, *A Brief Treatise upon Constitutional and Party Questions, and the History of Political Parties, As I Received It Orally from the Late Senator Stephen A. Douglas of Illinois* (D. Appleton and Company, New York, 1866), 150–154.

the old issues which divided the two parties, and were alike afraid to take either side of the Texas question, for fear of giving the other the advantage. Mr. Clay had been spending the winter with his friend Dr. Mercer in New Orleans, and in the months of March and April made a tour through the Southern States, on his way to Washington and Baltimore, to attend the Whig National Convention. When he arrived at Raleigh, in North Carolina, he remained a few days, where he was met by Mr. Crittenden and other friends from Washington, who it was understood and believed bore assurances from Silas Wright and Mr. Benton, in behalf of Mr. Van Buren, that if he, Mr. Clay, would take moderate grounds against the annexation of Texas, and especially would ignore it in the approaching Presidential election, he, Mr. Van Buren, in behalf of the Democratic party, and already regarded as virtually the nominee, would do the same thing, and thus the leaders of the two great parties would crush our Tylerism and Calhounism, by ignoring the Texas question, and having a fair fight upon the old issues of their respective parties. Accordingly, Mr. Clay published at Raleigh his celebrated letter upon the annexation of Texas, and a few days afterwards Mr. Van Buren published at Kinderhook a similar letter upon the same question. While Mr. Clay had sufficient control over the Whig party to induce them to accept the issue which he had made, Mr. Van Buren's letter created a general revolt in the Democratic ranks. In Virginia, the State central committee was immediately assembled, and released the delegates from that State from their instructions to support Mr. Van Buren, there not being time to call a State convention for that purpose. The example of Virginia was followed in other States, . . . New candidates came into the field, springing up on all sides, ready to pledge themselves to the annexation of Texas, and joined in the general cry against Van Buren. . . . Mr. Van Buren received a majority of the votes on several ballots, but less than two-thirds, when his vote became less and less, until he was withdrawn; when his friends, with a view of defeating the nomination of General Cass, who was the strongest candidate against him, and whom they regarded as the chief instrument in organizing the opposition to him, presented the name of James K. Polk, of Tennessee, having a letter already in their possession, committing him to the annexation of Texas. Mr. Polk was nominated by a large majority, by a union of a portion of the friends of Texas with the Van Buren men.

The nomination of Mr. Polk, with his known position in favor of *firm, high ground* against the pretensions of England in the Oregon question, made these two leading issues in the election, and enabled him to defeat Mr. Clay.

2. Resolution adopted by the Democratic National Convention in Baltimore, June, 1844:[17]

Resolved, That our title to the whole of the territory of Oregon is clear and unquestionable; and that no portion of the same ought to be ceded to England, or any other Power; and that the re-occupation of Oregon, and the re-annexation of Texas at the earliest practical period, and great American measures, which this convention recommends to the ardent support of the Democracy of the Union.

3. One of the most widely circulated pieces of campaign literature in 1844 was a letter written by Robert J. Walker, Senator from Mississippi:[18]

[The annexation of Texas] is not a question of the extension of

---

[17] *Congressional Globe*, 29th Cong., 1st Sess., Appendix, 694.

[18] *Letter of Mr. Walker, of Mississippi, Relative to the Reannexation of Texas: in Reply to the Call of the People of Carroll County, Kentucky, to Communicate His Views on That Subject* (Mifflin and Parry, Philadelphia, 1844), 8–9.

our limits, but of the restoration of former boundaries. It proposes no new addition to the valley of the Mississippi; but of its reunion, and all its waters, once more, under our dominion. If the Creator had separated Texas from the Union by mountain barriers, the Alps or the Andes, these might be plausible objections; but he has planed down the whole valley, including Texas, and united every atom of the soil and every drop of the waters of the mighty whole. He has linked their rivers with the great Mississippi, and marked and united the whole for the dominion of one government and the residence of one people; and it is impious in man to attempt to dissolve this great and glorious Union. Texas is a party of Kentucky, a portion of the same great valley. It is a part of New York and Pennsylvania, a part of Maryland and Virginia, and Ohio, and of all the western states, whilst the Tennessee unites with it the waters of Georgia, Alabama, and Carolina. . . . The treaty [Adams-Onís of 1819] which struck Texas from the Union, inflicted a blow upon this mighty valley. And who will say that the West shall remain dismembered and mutilated, and that the ancient boundaries of the republic shall never be restored? Who will desire to check the young eagle of America, now refixing her gaze upon our former limits, and repluming her pinions for her returning flight? What American will say, that the flag of the Union shall never wave again throughout that mighty territory; and that what Jefferson acquired, and Madison refused to surrender, shall never be restored? Who will oppose the reestablishment of our glorious constitution over the whole of the mighty valley which once was shielded by its benignant sway? Who will wish again to curtail the limits of this great republican empire, and again to dismember the glorious valley of the West . . . ?

4. *Niles' National Register* of October 12, 1844, recorded political

activity on the part of the Democrats in New York:[19]

The "Democratic" Mass Meeting at N. York, held last week, the papers of the party represent as being the largest political meeting ever held in that city. The *Herald* says,

"The annals of political excitement do not, we believe, present anything like a parallel to the scene presented. Long before the hour appointed for the meeting, Tammany Hall was densely crowded, and many thousands of the 'bone and sinew' thronged the park and the adjoining streets. There could not have been less than fifty thousand persons in the neighborhood of Tammany Hall during the evening, in attendance on the various meetings.

". . . Never has such a scene been witnessed in this city. The torches — the banners — the crowds — the shouting — the great flags streaming across Chatham Street — the violent gesticulations of the orators as the glare of the lamps and torches fell upon them — the hurrying to and fro of the vast crowds — the thundering cheers from old Tammany — all made up one of the most exciting scenes of popular enthusiasm which we have ever seen."

"The first speaker was George Bancroft, esq., the "democratic" candidate for governor of Massachusetts. The enthusiasm with which he was received altogether baffles description . . .

". . . For the vindication of our territory in its full extent, the merchants, and manufacturers, and agriculturists are equally interested. The harbors of Oregon are for American ships; its markets for American labor; its soil for the American ploughs; its wide domain for American institutions and American independence. [Terrific cheering — and shouts of 'Oregon is ours and must be ours' — 'Yes, and Texas, too,' and so on.]

"Mr. Bancroft proceeded to discuss the reannexation of Texas, contending that Texas is independent as a consequence of its existence, as having been but a temporary member of a confed-

19 *Niles' National Register,* October 12, 1844, 85, 86.

eracy, which military despotism had dissolved. He developed concisely the relations on the subject towards England and Mexico. He contended that the federative system was strengthened by its extension; that the system was destined, like the doctrine of democratic equality, to make the tour of the globe. . . ."

5. Commentary appearing in the *New Orleans Picayune* early in 1844:[20]

"Whar, I say *whar* is the individual who would give the first foot, the first outside shadow of a foot of the great Oregon? There aint no such individual. Talk about treaty occupations to a country over which the great American eagle has flown! I scorn treaty occupation. Who wants a parcel of low flung, 'outside barbarians,' to go in cahoo with us, and share alike a piece of land that always was and always will be ours? Nobody. Some people talk as though they were affeerd of England. Who's affeerd? Hav'nt we licked her twice, and can't we lick her again? Lick her! yes; jist as easy as a bar can slip down a fresh peeled saplin. . . ."

6. Letter dated August 28, 1844, from Andrew Jackson to Moses Dawson, which was published in *Niles' National Register*, October 5, 1844, at the height of the election campaign.[21]

Dear Sir: I am in possession of your note of the 27th . . . and although greatly enfeebled by the excessive warm weather of this month, shall endeavor to reply to it.

The more I have reflected on the policy of annexing Texas to the United States, the more decided is my conviction, that since the establishment of the federal constitution, no question has arisen of so great importance to the welfare and safety of the

[20] *Niles' National Register,* April 20, 1844, 114.
[21] *Niles' National Register,* October 5, 1844, 75, **76.**

people of the United States. It seems to me that in this instance, as in the revolution and our last war with Great Britain, kind Providence still interposes to help on our efforts in the cause of self-government, and to give us the necessary guarantee for our independence. . . .

There are many other aspects in which it can be made manifest that England will injure the United States, if it [the annexation of Texas] is rejected. But they are too obvious to bring to your notice. Take those already noted — take the question as it stands — the indisposition of the United States to profit by them is the most remarkable event that has occurred in history. No nation, under similar circumstances, has committed such an error. If there be patriotism in the effort to increase the wealth and happiness of all classes in our society — to diffuse the blessings of equal laws, and a just government — if there be love in the spirit which finds in this free land of ours the means to spread the light of the Gospel, and to teach fallen man throughout the world how he may recover his right to civil and religious liberty — it seems to me that all this patriotism — all this philanthropy — all this religion — appeals to us in favor of the addition of Texas to our Union.

7. Representative Andrew Johnson, Democrat from Tennessee, later to become governor of that state and subsequently President of the United States, made a speech on January 31, 1846:[22]

Mr. [Johnson] said he knew of no better figure to illustrate Texas and the United States by than the one suggested by General [Sam] Houston in a letter of his to General [Andrew] Jackson, which was published in the correspondence had between the two Governments. In that letter Texas was represented as a "bride adorned for her espousal;" meaning, he supposed, that Texas was willing to unite in wedlock with the United States, or Uncle Sam,

22 *Congressional Globe*, 29th Cong., 1st Sess., 334–335.

as he is sometimes called. . . . Mr. J. then proceeded to say that Uncle Sam, with his stars and stripes in his right hand, was seen approaching in the distance; as he drew near the altar, Texas, the interesting young virgin of the South, was seen leaning on his arm, the ring of "annexation" on her finger, and her countenance indicating that she had confessed that she had loved, and blushed that she had owned it. They stood before the altar; and whom found we there? James K. Polk, the political high priest, with the license in his hand, ready to pronounce the marriage ceremony. The Union is consummated. . . . *Uncle Sam and Texas* are conducted to the marriage chamber, and there, in the arms of affection, multiply and become exceedingly fruitful.

But now, shall his back be turned on her twin-sister? . . . *Uncle Sam* had lost none of his devotion to her twin-sister; he was still determined warmly as ever to afford her that protection which he had vowed; he was still for adopting the daughter of the North. . . . Prejudices might be attempted to be excited; new party lines might be attempted to be drawn; politicians might seek to make political capital; but the public opinion would bring Oregon in. The people were for it. If he were James K. Polk, (and he did not pretend to attempt to advise him,) while these little cliques — while these little germs of new parties were forming — he would run out his largest locomotive; he would get the steam up, he would put on the wood, and take in the water, and hitch in the Oregon car; and those who attempted to resist it he would crush in its ownward progress. The people would sustain him in it; the people were for it; the people will have it.

8. Henry Clay's Raleigh Letter, dated April 17, 1844:[23]

Subsequent to my departure from Ashland, in December last,

[23] Calvin Colton, *The Life, Correspondence, and Speeches of Henry Clay,* III (A. S. Barnes & Co., New York, 1857), 25, 26, 27, 28, 29.

I received various communications from popular assemblages and private individuals, requesting an expression of my opinion upon the question of the annexation of Texas to the United States. . . . The rejection of the overture of Texas, some years ago, to become annexed to the United States, had met with general acquiescence. Nothing had since occurred materially to vary the question. I had seen no evidence of a desire being entertained, on the part of any considerable portion of the American people, that Texas should become an integral part of the United States. . . . To the astonishment of the whole nation, we are now informed that a treaty of annexation has been actually concluded, and is to be submitted to the senate for its consideration.

The motives for my silence, therefore, no longer remain, and I feel it to be my duty to present an exposition of my views and opinions upon the question. . . .

. . . If, without the loss of national character, without the hazard of foreign war, with the general concurrence of the nation, without any danger to the integrity of the Union, and without giving an unreasonable price for Texas, the question of annexation were presented, it would appear in quite a different light from that in which, I apprehend, it is now to be regarded.

. . . Annexation and war with Mexico are identical. Now, for one, I certainly am not willing to involve this country in a foreign war for the object of acquiring Texas. I know there are those who regard such a war with indifference and as a trifling affair, on account of the weakness of Mexico, and her inability to inflict serious injury upon this country. But I do not look upon it thus lightly. . . .

Assuming that the annexation of Texas is war with Mexico, is it competent to the treaty-making power to plunge this country into war, not only without the concurrence of, but without deigning to consult congress, to which, by the constitution, belongs exclusively the power of declaring war.

I have hitherto considered the question upon the supposition that the annexation is attempted without the assent of Mexico. If she yields her consent, that would materially affect the foreign aspect of the question, if it did not remove all foreign difficulties. On the assumption of that assent, the question would be confined to the domestic considerations which belong to it. . . . I do not think that Texas ought to be received into the Union, as an integral part of it, in decided opposition to the wishes of a considerable and respectable portion of the confederacy. . . .

It is useless to disguise that there are those who espouse and those who oppose the annexation of Texas upon the ground of the influence which it would exert, in the balance of political power, between two great sections of the Union. I conceive that no motive for the acquisition of foreign territory would be more unfortunate, or pregnant with more fatal consequences, than that of obtaining it for the purpose of strengthening one part against another part of the common confederacy. Such a principle, put into practical operation, would menace the existence, if it did not certainly sow the seeds of a dissolution of the Union. It would be to proclaim to the world an insatiable and unquenchable thirst for foreign conquest or acquisition of territory. For if today Texas be acquired to strengthen one part of the confederacy, tomorrow Canada may be required to add strength to another. . . .

9. *Niles' National Register* reported the sentiments of the Vermont legislature in October, 1844:[24]

Vermont, The legislature of the state adjourned October 13, The select committee on slavery and the Texas question made a report, concluding with resolutions protesting against the extension of slavery, and against the annexation of Texas, which were passed — Ayes, 120; noes, 48. . . .

[24] *Niles' National Register,* December 7, 1844, 211.

10. Representative Caleb Blood Smith, Whig from Indiana, spoke on January 8, 1845:[25]

How is this change [for Texas annexation] to be accounted for? What has produced such a revolution in public sentiment? What new lights have been brought to bear upon this question, which have created such marvellous popularity for a measure, which, but so short a time since, was an object of aversion? Sir, there is no mystery in all this. It presents but another and a striking instance of the irresistible influence of party spirit and party discipline. The appliances of party have been brought to bear upon this question. The annexation of Texas has been incorporated into the democratic creed. The "lone star" has found a place upon the democratic banners. The faithful have been invoked to come up to the rescue, while the doom of the traitor has been denounced upon all who falter or waver in their support of this new article in the democratic confession of faith. The history of the last fifteen years has furnished us striking evidence of the power and influence of party spirit in shaping public opinion upon political questions.

11. During the next two years the issues and events of the election of 1844 were discussed frequently in Congress. Senator William Seger Archer, Whig from Virginia, spoke on March 18, 1846:[26]

. . . The Baltimore convention! What was it? . . . This body, really self-appointed, or nearly so, convened for an alleged specific object, to carry into effect an assumed public sentiment in relation to that object. Its *first proceeding* had been to discard the ad- mitted public sentiment which it purported to have met to effec-

25 *Congressional Globe*, 28th Cong., 2d Sess., Appendix, 78.
26 *Congressional Globe*, 29th Cong., 1st Sess., Appendix, 524.

tuate. . . . A junto, with no authority of any kind, or acting in admitted contradiction and violation of its professed authority, had been successful in dictating its most important election to the country; and its authority was now employed, on the *prestige* of that success, to dictate the legislation of the country on a subject of the most vital importance. This was the first open avowal the country had ever known of *Jacobinism* in its halls of legislation. It was yet to be seen how the avowal would be received.

12. Representative Abraham Robinson McIlvaine, Whig from Pennsylvania, spoke on January 25, 1845:[27]

How was it in Pennsylvania? Was Texas, immediate and unconditional, made the issue there? True, you might here and there see the "lone star" floating over our own stars and stripes. You might occasionally see a banner upon which was inscribed Polk, Dallas, Texas, and Oregon: but nowhere was Texas alone, Texas, immediately and unconditionally, presented as one of the issues. "Polk, Dallas, and a protective tariff," "Polk, Dallas, and the tariff of '42," "Polk, Dallas, and no United States Bank" — these were the issues presented by the democratic party. And now, votes thus fraudulently obtained, under false pretenses, are placed to the account of this Texas measure.

13. Representative John Strother Pendleton, Whig from Virgina, commented as follows in January, 1846:[28]

It was said early in the discussion that this Oregon question and that of Texas were "born and cradled" in the Baltimore Democratic Convention of 1844 — "twins," as my honorable friend from Massachusetts says; *two*, he might with more precise accuracy

[27] *Congressional Globe*, 28th Cong., 2d Sess., Appendix, 372.
[28] *Congressional Globe*, 29th Cong., 1st Sess., Appendix, 141.

have said, out of a very numerous litter of as monstrous political absurdities as any conclave, by so rapid a parturition, ever spawned upon the world.

14. The Election Results of 1844:[29]

	POLK	CLAY
POPULAR VOTE	1,338,464	1,300,097
ELECTORAL VOTE	POLK	CLAY
Maine	9	
New Hampshire	6	
Massachusetts		12
Rhode Island		4
Connecticut		6
Vermont		6
New York	36	
New Jersey		7
Pennsylvania	26	
Delaware		3
Maryland		8
Virginia	17	
North Carolina		11
South Carolina	9	
Georgia	10	
Alabama	9	
Mississippi	6	
Louisiana	6	
Tennessee		13
Kentucky		12
Ohio		23
Indiana	12	
Illinois	9	
Missouri	6	
Michigan	5	
Arkansas	3	
	170	105

[29] *Niles' National Register*, December 21, 1844, 243.

D. Post-Election Settlements in Texas

After James K. Polk won the presidential election of 1844 on a platform calling for the annexation of Texas and occupation of all of Oregon, President Tyler made a bold move. He recommended that Congress pass a joint resolution which would admit Texas into the Union. Such action required only a majority vote of both houses of Congress in contrast to the two thirds required by the Senate on a treaty. The House of Representatives responded with approval of the resolution on January 25, 1845, by a vote of 120 to 98. The Senate concurred on February 27, 27 to 25. Tyler signed the resolution on March 1, 1845—only three days before Polk became President!

As you read this section on the debates over annexation, attempt to determine the impact of the idea of Manifest Destiny as contrasted with other factors.

1. President John Tyler sent the following communication to the Senate on April 24, 1844:[30]

Washington, April 22, 1844

To the *Senate of the United States:*

. . . The country thus proposed to be annexed has been settled principally by persons from the United States, who emigrated on the invitation of both Spain and Mexico, and who carried with them into the wilderness which they have partially reclaimed the laws, customs, and political and domestic institutions of their native land. They are deeply indoctrinated in all the principles of civil liberty, and will bring along with them in the act of reassociation devotion to our Union and a firm and inflexible resolution to assist in maintaining the public liberty unimpaired — a

[30] James D. Richardson, ed., *A Compilation of the Messages and Papers of the Presidents, 1789–1897,* 53rd Cong., 2d Sess., Mis. Doc. 210, pt. 4, 308, 312.

consideration which, as it appears to me, is to be regarded as of no small moment. The country itself thus obtained is of incalculable value in an agricultural and commercial point of view. To a soil of inexhaustible fertility it unites a genial and healthy climate, and is destined at a day not distant to make large contributions to the commerce of the world. . . .

. . . I repeat, the Executive saw Texas in a state of almost hopeless exhaustion, and the question was narrowed down to the simple proposition whether the United States should accept the boon of annexation upon fair and even liberal terms, or, by refusing to do so, force Texas to seek refuge in the arms of some other power, either through a treaty of alliance, offensive and defensive, or the adoption of some other expedient which might virtually make her tributary to such power and dependent upon it for all future time. . . .

2. The *Houston Telegraph and Texas Register* of March 26, 1845:[31]

. . . But the motives which incline Texas to favor annexation at present, are the same which have governed all nations in all ages of the world. They are ('tis idle to conceal it) self-interest and self-preservation. Annexation is not sought as a new and interesting experiment in the art of Government. It is not desired as a partial relief from temporary evils, nor still for the aggrandizement of any political party. But from an overpowering sense of dire *necessity*. . . .

The sad experience of nine years of independent sovereignty has given us a foretaste of what we must assuredly undergo as an independent State. It has convinced the people that we are too

---

[31] *Houston Telegraph and Texas Register,* March 26, 1845.

weak to hold any thing but a subordinate and insignificant rank among other nations, that we are at the mercy of every stronger neighbor, and that though we may through the charity of other nations be permitted to exist, it must be in a state of contemptible dependence more galling to Freemen than tyranny itself.

3. An episode in the Texas legislature at the time the United States Senate debated the annexation of Texas as reported by the _Houston Telegraph and Texas Register_, February 19, 1845:[32]

Legislative Frolic — A few days before the close of the late session of Congress the members of the House of Representatives having become weary of the dull routine of reading and re-reading, amending and destroying bills, concluded to engage in a little harmless passtime. A bill had been introduced by Capt. Robert, setting forth a plan for the conquest of Mexico. — The members organized themselves into a committee of the whole upon this bill. The Captain solicited and obtained permission to address the committee on the importance of the measure, and made one of his best speeches, in which he detailed the means by which he expected to extend the arms of the Republic from mountain to mountain, and from river to river, until finally the Anglo-Saxon race and "honest Bob" also, should revel in the halls of the Montezumas. The members listened to this harrangue with all the gravity of Indian warriors, assembled around a council fire to listen to the war song of a noted chief. After the Captain had concluded his remarks one of the members rose, and submitted an amendment proposing that the territory of Texas should not extend merely to the boundaries of Mexico but to the Isthmus of Darien. Another proposed that it should extend to the Straits of Magellan. To these amendments the Captain did not object: but

[32] _Houston Telegraph and Texas Register_, February 19, 1845.

at length a member rose, and proposed that the whole of Ethiopia should be annexed to Texas, that the Captain should have his name changed to Napoleon the Third, and that he should marry the princess of Ethiopia, whose name should be changed to Annexus — that [he] should have a coat of arms, emblazoned upon it should be a buzzard soaring in a field of Oyute as if in contempt of a dead mustang beneath him . . . The committee finding that the frolic had gone too far, rose at once, reported the bill with amendments and recommended that it should be indefinitely postponed. . . .

4. Letter dated May 28, 1844, from John C. Calhoun to Francis Wharton:[33]

As to myself, I am of the impression, if we shall have the folly or wickedness to permit Great Britain to plant the lever of her power between the U. States and Mexico, on the Northern shore of the Gulph of Mexico, we give her a place to stand on, from which she can [brave?] at pleasure the American Continent and control its destiny. There is not a vacant spot left on the Globe, not excepting Cuba, to be seized by her, so well calculated to further the boundless schemes of her ambition and cupidity. If we should permit her to seize on it, we shall deserve the execration of posterity. Reject the treaty, and refuse to annex Texas, and she will certainly seize on it. A treaty of alliance commercial and political will be forthwith proposed by Texas to her, and I doubt not accepted. . . .

5. Representative James Butler Bowlin, Democrat from Missouri,

[33] American Historical Association, *Annual Report*, II (1899, Washington), 594.

spoke on the issue on January 15, 1845:[34]

. . . Let them reject Texas because she is a slave State, and are their domestic institutions changed by that act? If slavery be the evil gentlemen fancy it, is it lessened by rejecting Texas? No; but, on the contrary, they are insuring its permanent spread. Admit Texas, and the Rio Bravo, under our own guidance, constitutes the limits of this institution. Reject her, and that destiny which has guided her to her present national position, and that energy and courage which have won for her her liberty, upon the battle-field, will guide and animate her people until her standard waves in triumph over the halls of the Montezumas. Many of our own people would join them in the crusade against intolerance, super-stition, and oppression. The balmy air and virgin soil of Texas invite them; and they would go —

> "Though perils did
> Abound as thick as thought could make them,
> And in forms more horrid" —

in search of the rich blessings of such a country. . . .

6. Representative George Alfred Caldwell, Democrat from Kentucky, declared on January 21, 1845:[35]

Again, there is a prospect of a war with that powerful nation [Great Britain]. She is claiming our territory in Oregon — in fact has possession of it — and I fear that the question cannot be settled by treaty. The evil day may be postponed; but my deliberate opinion is that, at last, the question must and will be settled by the arbitrament of the sword. England has declared her intention

[34] *Congressional Globe*, 28th Cong., 2d Sess., Appendix, 95.
[35] *Congressional Globe*, 28th Cong., 2d Sess., Appendix, 151.

to endeavor to procure the abolition of slavery in Texas; and Texas may fall a prey to her stratagems, as millions have in other parts of the earth. Now let us suppose (and it is highly probable) that England, when she has her train completely laid, should force us into a war with her about Oregon. Already her battlements are erected and her cannon planted all along our northern and north-eastern boundary, in Nova Scotia, New Brunswick, and Canada. She will be in close alliance with Texas, and would find means, as she ever has done, to excite to hostilities the savage tribes of Indians, stretching from Canada to Texas, on our western frontier. . . .

7. Representative Isaac Edward Holmes, Democrat from South Carolina, spoke on January 14, 1845:[36]

At present, under the restrictive system, South Carolina receives eight millions for her produce; the expenses are still five millions, and her net income is only three millions. But if you reject Texas the evil will be increased. Texas cottons will meet us in Liverpool with a discrimination of 17 per cent. against us. It must further cripple our resources. But the evil will not end here. The West will get their supplies through Texas, and therefore the North will have no other markets than the South; the South being compelled to purchase of her, because the transit of goods from Texas across the Mississippi, and thence across the mountains, with all the difficulties of the contraband trade, will render British or Texian goods as dear on the seacoast as northern goods. But, as the North will then have us in their power, they will strive to balance the losses, as far as practicable, by levying further tribute upon us; and we of the South shall then pay higher prices for what we consume, and receive less prices for what we sell. We shall,

[36] *Congressional Globe*, 28th Cong., 2d Sess., Appendix, 107.

indeed, become the shorn lamb, without any tempering of the north winds.

8. Speech by Representative Moses Norris, Jr., Democrat from New Hampshire, on January 24, 1845:[37]

Sir, I believe that the resolutions of my State [New Hampshire] are strictly true, when they declare that the annexation of Texas will add more free than slave States to the Union. The soil, climate, and products of the larger portion of this territory are in nowise adapted to slave labor. The cotton, sugar, and rice lands along the Gulf of Mexico, embrace almost the whole extent upon which such labor can be profitably employed. A country adapted and devoted to the farming, manufacturing, and mechanical interests, cannot, and will not, sustain the institution of slavery for any great length of time. It soon becomes an insufferable burden, dwarfs away, sickens and dies. . . .

9. Speech on January 7, 1845, by Representative William Lowndes Yancey, a cotton planter, editor of the *Cahawba Democrat and Gazette*, later a "fire-eater" and Democrat from Alabama:[38]

. . . Like that mysterious star which of old drew the shepherds' attention from their lowly pursuits to the spot where the Savior of the world lay bandaged in his swaddling clothes, is this question now culminating over an infant republic, appealing to us as freemen, and as patriots, to forego our petty wrangling — to arise and accomplish in harmony the great destiny to which our principles have devoted us — the spread of the blessings of civilized freedom.

[37] *Congressional Globe*, 28th Cong., 2d Sess., Appendix, 189.
[38] *Congressional Globe*, 28th Cong., 2d Sess., Appendix, 86.

10. Speech by Representative Jacob Brinkerhoff, Democrat from Ohio, who later became a Republican, on January 13, 1845:[39]

. . . There were few gentlemen here but knew the advantage of having a great West to go to; where, away from the spirit of monopoly, the effects of family influence, the power of associated wealth, and the thousand other adverse influences which met a young man in the eastern portion of the Union, and kept down his efforts at achieving an independence, or treading with success the pathway of an honorable ambition; where none of these hinderances were in his way, but where there was ample room. . . .

11. Speech by Representative Andrew Johnson, Democrat from Tennessee, on January 21, 1845:[40]

. . . [The Texans] have gone out from their mother country, as the twelve spies in old times. They have succeeded in exploring and possessing themselves of the only remaining portion of Canaan destined by God for his American Israel. Having accomplished the great object of their mission, they now return, not as prodigals, whose estates had been wasted in riotous living, or with even specimens of the production of their delightful country, but with the country itself — sufficient in extent to make an empire: and this country they are willing to lay down at our feet. Will we refuse their admission into our family of States? They are our kindred and our blood! our brothers and our sisters! — have they not proved themselves worthy of being associated with their own noble race?

12. Speech by Representative John Wooleston Tibbotts, a Democrat

[39] *Congressional Globe,* 28th Cong., 2d Sess., Appendix, 121.
[40] *Congressional Globe,* 28th Cong., 2d Sess., Appendix, 223.

from Kentucky and supporter of expansion, on May 7, 1844:[41]

The value of Texas — a country so rich in the fertility of its soil — so intimately connected with this country by its rivers and outlets, and other natural relations — so necessary to the protection and defence, and as a key to the great pass to the settlement of our Territory of Oregon — so essential to the safety of New Orleans, the great mart of our western and southern commerce, and to the maritime command of the Gulf of Mexico, which Englishmen already have boasted in Parliament belongs to them, and declare must be maintained by them, — cannot be estimated. It will open a vast market for the agricultural productions and manufactures of the West and of the East, protected from foreign competition. It will secure to us the control of the great staple of cotton, for which England is dependent upon us, and by which she saves her toiling millions from starvation, and by giving them employment, prevents them from rebellion against her oppressive system of taxation. It will be greatly to the interest of the commercial enterprise of the Northern States, and of New England in particular, and of the manufacturing and agricultural districts of this country, and may put an end to this great bone of contention — the tariff — by opening to us an almost unlimited home market for our manufacturers. . . . It would place all the Indian tribes which swarm upon our western borders under our immediate control. It will extend the principles of civil liberty, for they march *pari passu* with the migrations of the Anglo-Saxon race. Above all, it will be favorable to the quieting of a question of the deepest interest to this country. . . . Sir, it will be favorable to the gradual, peaceable, and constitutional abolition of slavery on this continent. The African race . . . will gradually recede from the

[41] *Congressional Globe*, 28th Cong., 1st Sess., Appendix, 450.

North, which is uncongenial to their natures. . . . They will flow peacefully in an increasing stream along the Mississippi, the great father of waters, and through this very land of Texas, until they end their pilgrimage on the shores of the Gulf, and in a climate congenial to their nature, and become blended with the mixed population of Mexico.

13. From *Niles' National Register*, February 1, 1845:[42]

"The Empire Club," at the city of New York, held a great meeting on the subject, on the 16 ult., and entered into resolutions characteristic of that body, demanding the immediate annexation of Texas in strong language, and deprecating any consideration of the slavery question on the occasion. The club adjourned to meet and unite with "the democracy of N. York at Tammany Hall, on Friday, the 24th of January, in full and bold expression of their sentiments in favor of annexation."

14. Letter from an irate "Texian" which appeared in November, 1844:[43]

Messrs. Editors: Since my arrival in this city I have heard that my friend Anson Jones has been elected president of the Texian republic. It is well known that he is opposed to annexation, and his election may be considered the expression of the public opinion of Texas on this subject.

The position of our Lone Star seems not to be understood in the United States. The desire manifested in the south to add Texas

[42] *Niles' National Register*, February 1, 1845, 352.
[43] *Niles' National Register*, November 30, 1844, 194.

to the union is not founded on any attachment to us. It results from pure selfishness, and the project is sustained, first, because it strengthens the institution of slavery; and, next, because it will give political power to the south, by the probable creation of several new states out of our immense territory. . . .

On the contrary, the establishment of a new republic would be a proof of the progress of freedom — a new illustration of the power of men to rule themselves by a representative form of government, and an example to the world of the strength of republican principles. Annex Texas to the union, and it is a confession of our weakness, of the feebleness of republican principles, and the necessity of our leaning upon some powerful nation for support.

A Texian

15. An article entitled "THE RE-ANNEXATION OF CANADA" appeared in the *Baltimore American* in 1845:[44]

It will be found that the reasons which are considered so potential in favor of the acquisition of Texas apply with equal if not greater force to the acquisition of Canada. *The National Intelligencer* has placed some of the arguments for the latter in the line of comparative analogy — thus:

Like the other, it will be a "re-annexation;" for Canada and the present United States were once parts of the same empire.

The acquisition of Canada will be a much more positive enlargement of the "area of freedom" than that of Texas; for Texas already enjoys a republican government, and Canada does not. . . .

It will be far more advantageous to our manufacturers; for Canada contains a vastly larger population than Texas.

[44] *Niles' National Register,* February 1, 1845, from the *Baltimore American,* 345.

The annexation of Canada will certainly be less hurtful to the cotton-planting states than that of Texas, for it will not bring in a competition in a production already excessive.

To the sugar-planters it will not oppose a rival; while it will give them an enlarged market.

Canada is not so fine a grain or stock-growing country as a large part of Texas is represented to be; and must therefore be a more advantageous acquisition to the west and northwest.

It will still better secure and perpetuate the peculiar institution, the protection of which is a main argument in favor of the other measure; for it will cut off the intercourse of England with all our part of this continent, and remove the refuge which has long existed in Canada for fugitive slaves.

16. Letter written in January, 1845, by Henry Hinsdale, clerk of the Society of Friends, after their annual meeting in New York:[45]

That your memorialist team, with regret, that it is proposed to annex the state of Texas to, and incorporate it with, the states of this Union; and, believing, as they do, that the consummation of this measure would extend and perpetuate slavery, and place in jeopardy that peace and harmony which now happily exist among the nations of the earth, they feel it to be an incumbent and religious duty respectfully, but earnestly, to demonstrate against such annexation.

17. *Niles' National Register* for February 8, 1845, included both a description of the Massachusetts Anti-Annexation Convention in

---

[45] *Niles' National Register*, February 1, 1845, 342–343, from *The National Intelligencer* of January 27, 1845.

Boston and a Texas commentary on the Massachusetts meeting:[46]

[Mr. Lovejoy stated] It had been said that the American people desired Texas. But that he denied — he denied that the American people wanted either Texas, its lands, or its runaway scoundrels. He denied, too, that the object was desired by either party, as a party. Whence, then, came the desire now so apparent?

Texas was wanted to extend the curse and the abominations of slavery, and it rested with us to say if we would approve the purpose. . . .

Of this meeting the *Houston Telegraph and Texas Register* of March 5, 1845, stated: "A convention was recently held at Fanuel Hall, Boston, by the opponents of Annexation. Great exertions were made to collect a large crowd and to induce influential men to attend the meeting: but in vain. The papers mention that the chief actors at this convention were abolition fanatics and knaves, and that they were not numerous, nor did they represent the worth, talents, property, nor the popular will of the State. . . .

18. Speech by Senator Daniel Webster, Whig from Massachusetts, on December 22, 1845:[47]

. . . In the first place, I have, on the deepest reflection, long ago come to the conclusion, that it was of very dangerous tendency and doubtful consequences to enlarge the boundaries of this Government, or the territories over which our laws are now estab-

[46] *Niles' National Register*, February 8, 1845, 363.

[47] Thomas Hart Benton, ed., *Abridgment of the Debates of Congress, from 1789 to 1856*, XV (D. Appleton and Company, New York, 1861), 296–297.

lished. There must be some limit to the extent of our territory, if we would make our institutions permanent. And in this permanency lies the great subject of all my political efforts, the paramount object of my political regard. The Government is very likely to be endangered, in my opinion, by a further enlargement of its already vast territorial surface.

In the next place, I have always wished that this country should exhibit to the nations of the earth the example of a great, rich, and powerful Republic, which is not possessed by a spirit of aggrandizement. It is an example, I think, due from us to the world, in favor of the character of republican government. . . .

. . . I never could, and never can, persuade myself to be in favor of the submission of other States into the Union as slave States, with the inequalities which were allowed and accorded to the slaveholding States then in existence by the constitution.

19. Speech by Senator Jacob Welsh Miller, Whig from New Jersey, on February 25, 1845. Also note the statement by Representative John Wooleston Tibbotts (Reading 12).[48]

The friends of annexation at the North present to us a very dissimilar view of the effect of this measure upon slavery. They tell us that they are opposed to slavery; that it is a national evil, only to be endured under the restraints of the constitution, and that they adopted this measure as a means of driving the evil further from them at present, and of finally extirpating it altogether from the country. The senator from Pennsylvania [Mr. James Buchanan] belongs to this latter class. That senator, in his speech delivered a few days since, said:

"I am not friendly to slavery in the abstract; and I look to Texas

---

[48] *Congressional Globe*, 28th Cong., 2d Sess., Appendix, 354.

as the probable means of relieving the Union from slavery at some distant day. . . ."

If I correctly understand the senator's plan for the abolition of slavery, it is by means of what may be called the draining system. Texas is to be the last grand reservoir into which each State will pour its stream of surplus slavery. The negro, through a thousand years of servile pilgrimage from generation to generation, is to drag his weary way from the Delaware to the Del Norte, exhausting, in his painful march, every field of labor by the sweat of his brow, until the whole race shall be congregated in one dark mass of worn out, profitless slaves, beneath the sunny skies of Texas. Then and there is to terminate the long and wearied march of slavery. The wilderness is passed; and from Pisgah's top the senator, in prophetic vision, beholds the tribes make their exodus over Jordan into the promised land of Mexico — "there (as the senator tells us) to enjoy their freedom without that taint of degradation which they must ever experience among the Anglo-American race."

What may be the destiny of our slave institutions, or even of the country itself, in a thousand years to come, is not for short-sighted mortals to predict; but I cannot conceive how we are to get rid of slavery through the process of annexing foreign slave States to the Union, by opening new and more profitable fields for its employment. Our slaves, I have no doubt, will pass into Mexico as they have passed into Texas; but they will go in company with their masters, the Anglo-American race, forming new slave States, hereafter to be admitted into the Union under the precedent we are now about to establish. . . .

20. Speech by Representative John T. Hardin, Whig from Illinois,

who was later killed at the Battle of Buena Vista, on January 15, 1845.[49]

One word in reference to an argument often repeated by the friends of annexation, that "if we don't take Texas Great Britain will." Should such an event be seriously contemplated, in my judgment the combined powers of the army and navy of this government should be used, if necessary, to prevent it. But there is not the least danger of such an occurrence. Great Britain is seeking to extend her dominions in another direction, amidst the densely settled portions of the Asiatic nations, where she can find a population to consume her manufacturers, and weak and cowardly tribes who are easily subjected to her dominion. . . .

. . . Some gentlemen boast of an enlarged and liberal patriotism, which constrains them to go for the extension of our dominion and our free institutions over the Territory of Texas, now that it is practicable. Why, sir, has not Texas a republican government like ours? And is she not capable of self-government? If not, it is certain that she is unfit to be annexed to our Union. But, sir, I insist upon gentlemen calling things by their right names. Patriotism consists in loving our own country, and not in thirsting after the soil of another. . . .

. . . But if we adopt Texas . . . I feel it imperative on me to inquire what is to be the result of such a policy?

. . . therefore we must make war upon England, and take from her Canada, Nova Scotia, and New Brunswick. After we have fairly thrashed that puny power and annexed all the country north of us to Baffin's bay and the Frozen Ocean, we will turn our warlike eyes to Cuba, which is the key of the Gulf of Mexico; and as that would be very convenient for us, we would forthwith

[49] *Congressional Globe*, 28th Cong., 2d Sess., Appendix, 274, 275, 276.

demolish the dominion of Spain in that fertile Island. That would be another opportunity, which should not be neglected, of "extending the area of freedom," by adding the vast numbers of slaves which abound in that island to the limited number in our southern States. Such a reannexation of the island to the continent would doubtless soothe the expansive patriotism of sundry overburdened patriots.

21. Speech by Representative Joshua R. Giddings, an antislavery Whig from Ohio:[50]

. . . But let us admit Texas, and we shall place the balance of power in the hands of the Texans. They, with the southern States, will control the policy and the destiny of this nation; our tariff will then be held at the will of the Texan advocates of free trade. Are our friends of the North prepared to deliver over this policy to the people of Texas? Are the liberty-loving democrats of Pennsylvania ready to give up the tariff? To strike off all protection from the articles of iron and coal and other productions of that State, in order to purchase a slave-market for their neighbors, who, in the words of Thomas Jefferson Randolph, "breed men for the market like oxen for the shambles?"

. . . Why not advise the people of our free States at once to leave their homes, to go to Texas, and become the voluntary "hewers of wood and drawers of water" to those fugitive criminals who, within the last fifteen years, were driven from the United States to avoid punishment for their crimes?

22. Speech by Representative Charles Hudson, Whig from Massachusetts, a Unitarian minister, a member of the state board of educa-

[50] Joshua R. Giddings, *Speeches in Congress* (John P. Jewett and Company, Boston, 1853), 100, 102, 106.

tion, later editor of the *Boston Daily Atlas,* on January 20, 1845:[51]

As this measure presents very little inducement to win the support of manufacturers, gentlemen hold it out as a boon to the agriculturists; they, too, are to get a great market in Texas. And what sort of a country is Texas? Why, according to these gentlemen, it is one of the most delightful regions on earth — a perfect paradise — a rich and fresh and fertile Eden — a territory as large as France, and furnishing a market for all the wheat and flour, and lard and meats, and breadstuffs of the West, which were to float down on the bosom of the father of waters, and be consumed in this garden of America — this all-prolific, all-consuming region! . . .

. . . The 117,000 poverty stricken people to furnish a market for all the northern and middle States! It is too ridiculous for serious consideration. . . .

23. Speech by Representative Robert Clarke Winthrop, Whig from Massachusetts, on January 6, 1845:[52]

. . . If it be alleged that the insurgents of Texas are emigrants from the United States, it is obvious to reply that, by their voluntary expatriation, of honor or infamy, they have forfeited all claim to our paternal regard. If it be true that they have left a land of freedom for a land of despotism, they have done it with their eyes open, and deserve their destiny. Perhaps this language is a little too severe; but I am clearly of opinion that men who have deserted their own country for a foreign soil, are not preeminently entitled to our freshest and most cordial sympathies. . . .

[51] *Congressional Globe,* 28th Cong., 2d Sess., Appendix, 335.
[52] *Ibid.,* p. 395.

24. Vote on the Joint Resolution for Annexation: The House of Representatives.[53]

	DEMOCRATS		WHIGS	
	YEAS	NAYS	YEAS	NAYS
Maine	1	4	0	2
New Hampshire	2	2	0	0
Massachusetts	1	1	0	8
Connecticut	3	1	0	0
Vermont	0	1	0	3
Rhode Island	0	0	0	2
New York	9	14	0	10
New Jersey	3	1	0	1
Pennsylvania	10	0	0	13
Delaware	0	0	0	1
Maryland	0	0	0	5
Virginia	10	0	1	3
North Carolina	5	0	0	4
South Carolina	7	0	0	0
Georgia	6	0	2	0
Alabama	6	0	1	0
Mississippi	4	0	0	0
Louisiana	4	0	0	0
Arkansas	1	0	0	0
Missouri	5	0	0	0
Kentucky	5	0	0	5
Tennessee	6	0	4	0
Ohio	9	2	0	10
Indiana	8	0	0	2
Illinois	6	0	0	1
Michigan	1	2	0	0
	112	28	8	70

[53] *Houston Telegraph and Texas Register*, February 19, 1845.

E. Post-Election Settlements in Oregon

President Polk in December, 1845, in keeping with his campaign promise of the previous year, asked Congress to grant him authority to terminate with England the treaty of joint occupation of Oregon. Polk, concerned about the possibility of war with Mexico due to conflicting claims to parts of Texas, did not seek a similar problem over Oregon. Great Britain agreed, so the two countries reached a compromise in June, 1846, whereby the United States and England agreed on the 49° parallel as a boundary.

As you read about the settlement of the Oregon question, attempt to determine the role played by the idea of a Manifest Destiny as contrasted with other factors.

1. From the inaugural address of James K. Polk, March 4, 1845.[54]

Nor will it become in a less degree my duty to assert and maintain by all constitutional means the right of the United States to that portion of our territory which lies beyond the Rocky Mountains. Our title to the country of the Oregon is "clear and unquestionable," and already are our people preparing to perfect that title by occupying it with their wives and children. But eighty years ago our population was confined on the west by the ridge of the Alleghanies. Within that period — within the lifetime, I might say, of some of my hearers — our people, increasing to many millions, have filled the eastern valley of the Mississippi, adventurously ascended the Missouri to its headsprings, and are

---

[54] *Inaugural Addresses of the Presidents of the United States from George Washington, 1789, to John F. Kennedy, 1961,* 87th Cong., 1st Sess., House Document No. 218, 97–98.

already engaged in establishing the blessings of self-government in valleys of which the rivers flow to the Pacific. The world beholds the peaceful triumphs of the industry of our emigrants. To us belongs the duty of protecting them adequately where they may be upon our soil. The jurisdiction of our laws and the benefits of our republican institutions should be extended over them in the distant regions which they have selected for their homes. The increasing facilities of intercourse will easily bring the States, of which the formation in that part of our territory can not be long delayed, within the sphere of our federative Union. In the meantime every obligation imposed by treaty or conventional stipulations should be sacredly respected.

2. Message dated December 2, 1845, from President Polk to the Senate:[55]

. . . For the protection of emigrants whilst on their way to Oregon, against the attacks of the Indian tribes occupying the country through which they pass, I recommend that a suitable number of stockades and block-house forts be erected along the usual route between our frontier settlements on the Missouri and the Rocky Mountains; and that an adequate force of mounted riflemen be raised to guard and protect them on their journey. The immediate adoption of these recommendations by Congress will not violate the provisions of the existing treaty. It will be doing nothing more for American citizens, than British laws have long since done for British subjects in the same territory.

❋ ❋ ❋ ❋ ❋ ❋

The rapid extension of our settlements over our territories here-

[55] Thomas Hart Benton, ed., *Abridgment of the Debates of Congress, from 1789 to 1856*, XV (D. Appleton and Company, New York, 1861), 251.

tofore unoccupied; the addition of our new States to our confederacy; the expansion of free principles, and our rising greatness as a nation, are attracting the attention of the powers of Europe; and lately the doctrine has been broached in some of them, of a "balance of power" on this continent, to check our advancement. The United States, sincerely desirous of preserving relations of good understanding with all nations, cannot in silence permit any European interference on the North American continent; and should any such interference be attempted, will be ready to resist it at any and all hazards.

3. Speech by Representative James J. Faran, Democrat from Ohio and Associate Editor of the *Cincinnati Enquirer*, 1844–1881, on April 14, 1846:[56]

. . . Let us first examine the offers that have been made and rejected by the parties respectively in their negotiations on this subject, in order to see how far Great Britain has committed herself in maintaining any particular position in this controversy.

BRITISH OFFERS — *October 6, 1818*

"That so much of the northwest coast of America as lies between the forty-fifth and forty-ninth parallels of latitude, with its harbors, &c., should be free and open to the citizens and subjects of the two Powers respectively, for the purposes of trade and commerce. This agreement not to prejudice the claims of either party to any territorial authority within those limits."

Rejected by our Government.

July 13, 1824

"That the boundary of the two Powers be designated by extend-

[56] *Congressional Globe*, 29th Cong., 1st Sess., Appendix, 610, 615–616.

ing the line of the forty-ninth parallel to the northeast branch of
the Columbia, thence down the same to the Pacific. The navigation of the Columbia to be free to the citizens and subjects of both
Powers."

This was rejected.

December 1, 1826

"That, in addition to the foregoing, the possession of Port Discovery, in the southern coast of De Fuca's Inlet, and a small strip
of country to be annexed thereto. Also, that no work should be
established on the Columbia to impede or hinder the free navigation thereof."

This was rejected.

August 26, 1844

"In addition to the previous offers of July 13, 1824, and December 1, 1823, to make free to the United States any port or ports
that the United States might desire, either on the main land or
on Vancouver's Island, south of latitude 49°."

This was rejected.

Offers by the United States — Sept. 17, 1818

"To extend the forty-ninth parallel of latitude to the Pacific
Ocean, with the navigation of all streams intersected by this line
and flowing into the Pacific, to be open and free to the citizens
and subjects of both Powers."

This was rejected by the British.

April 2, 1824

"Mr. Rush proposed to continue the third article of the treaty
of October 20, 1818, with the additional clause that no settlement

should be made by American citizens north of the fifty-first parallel of latitude, nor by British subjects either south of the fifty-first degree or north of the fifty-fifth degree of north latitude."

This was rejected.

July 13, 1824

"Mr. Rush proposed to modify the foregoing by substituting the forty-ninth parallel of latitude for the fifty-first."

This was rejected.

November 15, 1826

"To extend the forty-ninth parallel to the Pacific, and if it intersected any branch of the Columbia navigable to the ocean, the navigation of such branch to be free to the citizens and subjects of both Powers."

This was rejected.

July 12, 1845

"To divide the Oregon territory by the forty-ninth parallel of north latitude, from the Rocky Mountains to the Pacific Ocean, and to make free to Great Britain any port or ports on Vancouver's Island, south of this parallel, which Great Britain might desire."

This was rejected.

* * * * * *

But sir, I will tell you why it is that the West takes such a deep interest in this matter. It is because we look upon it as a national question. . . . The people of the West love the whole country and that makes them ardent in its defence; they believe our title to the whole of Oregon good. . . . They do not want to see any foreign Power occupy any portion of American territory, much less

Great Britain, whom they are slow to forget. For they cannot but recollect their perpetual enemy, who has been the instigator of nearly all the Indian outrages that have covered almost every square league of the West with the blood of its men, women, and children. An enemy who even now, to intimidate us from asserting our rights to the Oregon territory, at the same time that he boasts of his refinement and Christian character, as if impelled by the instincts of his nature, openly intimates that, should war come, he will invite the negroes of the South to murder their masters, and will also burn the cities on our seaboard; . . .

4. Speech by Representative J. D. Cummins, Democrat from Ohio, on February 7, 1846:[57]

But, sir, where is Oregon, and what is it? Oregon is that part of the North American continent which lies between the Mexican line, on the 42d parallel of north latitude, and the Russian line, on the parallel of 54° 40′ north latitude. It is bounded on the west by the Pacific ocean, and on the east by the Rocky Mountains — upon which line it is, the greater part of the way, coterminous with the other territories of the United States. It embraces about nine hundred miles of the western coast of this continent bordering on the Pacific ocean, is of an average width of about six hundred miles, and contains about four hundred thousand square miles of territory. In extent, it embraces more territory than the "Old Thirteen States" on the Atlantic slope. Its climate is much milder, and more genial than the climate in the same latitude on the Atlantic; its soil is fertile, its streams pure, its forests are abundantly supplied with the choicest timber; and, in short, it possesses the elements of a great and valuable country.

[57] *Congressional Globe*, 29th Cong., 1st Sess., Appendix, 411–412.

If we do our duty in preserving and maintaining our just rights there, Oregon is destined to be the home of millions of happy and prosperous freemen, whose labors will be rewarded by the exuberant fertility of its valleys and whose flocks and herds will feed upon its thousand hills. As a means of our military defence, it is a tower of strength, both by land and sea. It skirts one whole front of this Republic, and hems us in on the west, and entirely shuts us out from the Pacific. It furnishes abundant supplies of timber, of which to construct navies, and great, capacious, and safe bays and harbors, in which they can float in safety. To any country possessing skill, industry, and enterprise, the possession of Oregon will give the military and marine control and supremacy of the Pacific ocean and its islands, of China, the East Indies, and the western coast of South America.

How long will it be before the commerce of the Atlantic and the Pacific will be connected across the continent by the avenues of trade? How long will it be before the iron arms of railroads will stretch from sea to sea? I have no doubt but there are thousands now living who will witness the consummation of that magnificent project. Sir, it is practicable, and the magnitude of the interests dependent upon it are too great to be permitted to lie dormant. The distance across this continent is variously estimated at from seventeen hundred to two thousand miles; take the greatest distance, and add to it one thousand miles for curvatures and deviations of a railroad, and you have a distance of three thousand miles. Cannot that distance be overcome? Why, sir, there are now in the United States, completed and in successful operation, over four thousand miles of railroad, and as much more projected, and large portions of it in an advanced state of completion. Do gentlemen doubt this? . . .

5. Speech by Representative Edward Dickinson Baker, Whig from Illinois, on January 29, 1846. Baker later participated in the siege of Vera Cruz and in 1860 became a Republican Senator from Oregon.[58]

[It] has been enforced in the declaration of a general principle, as in the declaration of Mr. Monroe, in 1823, "That the American continents are henceforth not to be considered as subjects for future colonization by any European Power"; it has been particularly and specifically relied on by the President of the United States in his Inaugural Address to the people and to the world; it has received his earnest and solemn sanction in the late Annual Message to Congress; it has been the subject of long and repeated negotiation. . . .

6. Speech by Representative Andrew Kennedy, Democrat from Indiana, on January 10, 1846.[59]

We, of the West, are not "bookish" men. What little education we have, we received after the labor of the day had been done, in the school of adversity, in the Far West, and almost on the verge of civilization, where our struggles have been with the Indian, and our wrestling with the bear — now no common occurrence. We have, therefore, left it to our agents to settle the question to whom, by the record, Oregon belongs. This they have done, and done well. Our part of the task, which is to maintain and defend our rights, is now to commence; and by the remembrance of the deeds of our fathers, and the strong affection we cherish of our fathers, and the strong affection we cherish for our wilderness-homes, we will defend them or perish in the attempt. We do not want war, and you slander us when you say that our

---

[58] *Congressional Globe*, 29th Cong., 1st Sess., Appendix, 151.
[59] *Congressional Globe*, 29th Cong., 1st Sess., Appendix, 209–210, 211.

hands are itching to grasp the steel of strife, and our hearts panting for the deadly conflict. No people more highly appreciate or value peace and brotherly love, that should bind in one unbroken chain all the families of man, than the people of the West. We know that our free institutions flourish best in the mild and genial atmosphere of peace; but, when it comes to the surrender of the patrimony of our fathers — to receding from, or yielding up our just rights upon soil, then, we say, peace can no longer be honorable; and *we* shall not hesitate when it comes to the question of *dishonorable peace,* or *honorable war.*

Some gentlemen scoff at what has been called the destiny of nations — or what is the same thing, the providence of God in the affairs of men. Sir, where were we two centuries ago? We were a handful of pilgrims landing upon Plymouth rock, and a small band of cavaliers planted on the sunny sands of the South. From this small beginning, and in this short time, what have we become? We have advanced by steady and peaceful strides, covering the continent with independent and industrious citizens, following up the red man foot by foot, driving him from haunt to haunt, until, like a small and broken cloud that skirts the far-off horizon, he now rests along the shores of the western ocean, ready to take his last plunge, and leave the graves of his fathers, to be visited no more forever. Is there no destiny in this? Is not the finger of God as plainly seen as when he first set in the heavens the star of Bethlehem? The man who sees it not must be either blind or infidel.

It is said by some that we do not need the Oregon territory for purposes of settlement. This is a great mistake; and that you may clearly see the error into which some have fallen, I invite you to go to the West, and visit one of our log cabins, and number its inmates. There you will see a strong, stout youth of eighteen, with his better half, just commencing the first struggles of independent life. Thirty years from that time, visit them again; and instead of two, you will find in that same family twenty-two. This is what I call the American multiplication table. Multiply this and the next generation by this table, and where, without Oregon, will you find room for our people? The greater portion of this multiplying mass of humanity have their faces turned towards the setting sun. "Westward ho!" is the cry; and you can no more stop them this side the shores of the Pacific than you can dam up the mighty waters of the Missouri, whilst the snows are melting on the Stony mountain in which it takes its rise. Where, I repeat, without Oregon, are we to find room for our people? What are we to do with the little white-headed girls and boys — God bless them! — who throng our western valleys, bright and blooming ones — the flowers that deck our illimitable prairies?

7. **Lewis Charles Levin was a founder of the American Party and one-time editor of the *Philadelphia Daily Sun*. He made the following speech while serving as a representative from Pennsylvania, January 9, 1846:[60]**

. . . I am one of those who do not believe "Oregon" to be the real cause of the present belligerent attitude of England. The controversy between us is rather to be traced to the conflict between feudal institutions and republican systems of government. Our example of free government is thought to be dangerous to the permanency of Europe's thrones; and England has been put forward, as she was in the case of republican France, to head the combination of kings against the cause of freedom. Our glorious flag . . . has at last awakened the monarchs of Europe to the danger that gleams from the majestic emblems of liberty. Let Europe combined, if she will, strike at the cause of American freedom, by

[60] *Congressional Globe*, 29th Cong., 1st Sess., Appendix, 95, 98.

making Oregon a pretext for war; there is a power in the free-
man's prayer that pales with fear the face of tyrants, and makes
them tremble on their thrones. . . . Here, as Americans, we battle
with nature on our side — here we do battle for freedom, or freedom's stage, with mountains for our shields, oceans for our garri-
sons, God himself for our ally! . . .

8. Speech by Representative John A. McClemand, Democrat from
Illinois, on January 8, 1846:[61]

Whilst England controls India, and all the routes of commerce,
as she now does, and trade to China continues to traverse the
long routes passing beneath the equator, American trade, elsewhere so thrifty, must continue to languish. . . .

Is the great enterprise of the American people then unequal,
in the face of this Russian success [trading with China], to the
small achievement of connecting the navigable waters of the
Missouri and Columbia, and prosecuting direct trade between the
valley of the Mississippi and . . . China? The memorial from
Oregon upon our tables informs us that already 10,000 Americans
have opened a wagon road from the Missouri to the Pacific;
that they have established a Government, made laws, and orig-
inated agriculture, commerce, and manufactures; that they have
erected there a domestic seaport upon our western seaboard.

9. Speech by Representative Cornelius Darragh, Whig from Pennsylvania, on February 9, 1846:[62]

. . . When our title [to Oregon] shall be made perfect, and our
possession asserted and maintained, the moral, the political, and

[61] *Ibid.*, 278.
[62] *Congressional Globe*, 29th Cong., 1st Sess., Appendix, 171.

the commercial affairs of Asia will be revolutionized. I believe that the man is now living who will see your Atlantic cities connected by railroad with the Pacific ocean. That accomplished and the trade of China, and India, and the islands of the Pacific rush by this course to Europe. Six or eight days, by railroad, will whirl you from some magnificent city, to be founded and built on the shores of the Pacific, to Philadelphia or New York. We shall be neighbors to the Chinese; and as it was from the East the nations of the world received their early knowledge of the arts and sciences, so from the west it shall be given back to them Ay, sir; not only their arts and sciences highly improved, but we will take to them the blessings and the republicanism of Christianity.

10. Speech by Representative William Sawyer, Democrat from Ohio, in answer to Representative Robert Clarke Winthrop (Reading 17):[63]

. . . The gentleman from Massachusetts, [Mr. Winthrop,] who spoke in the early part of this debate, asked very significantly where we find our title to this territory, and whether it may not be found in some corner of Adam's will? No; it dates further back — long before Adam's dust was fashioned into man; our title dates with the creation of the world. We received it from high Heaven — from destiny, if you please. In the course of events, in the progress and consummation of this destiny, Christopher Columbus was sent across the ocean to examine this country, and he found that it was good for man to dwell upon. By-and-by, our fathers followed and took possession; here they established the seat of empire; here they sowed the seeds of democracy, which sprang up and brought forth abundance of excellent fruit. But the prosperity of this country soon excited the jealousy and fears of another people, and they sent armies to subjugate it to their

[63] *Congressional Globe,* 29th Cong., 1st Sess., Appendix, 227, 228–229.

wn will and control. There rose one George Washington, who drove the invaders from the land, and located his family upon t. Columbus and Washington were but the agents Heaven employed to place us in possession of our own. This is our claim of title, and I can see no defect in it. I contend it is good and sufficient against all other claimants. This island — or, if you prefer to call it so, this continent — was made and set apart for our especial benefit. We have a right to every inch of it, and it would be ingratitude to high Heaven to surrender a single pebble. . . .

11. The *Washington Madisonian* commented on United States claims to Oregon:[64]

But let [Great Britain] do it — let her try it without a day's notice, if she chooses — she will find us armed and equipped according to law. She will find, to her cost, that the mantle of the immortal hero, who still lingers at the Hermitage, has fallen upon one who is fully able to preserve from blemish the standard of our nation's honor. The venerable trunk may decay — but the *Young Hickory* tree defies alike, in the unscathed greatness of its strength, the tornado's violence and the red lightning's wrath. We calmly, coolly, and dispassionately, say to Old England, that Oregon is our property; we own it, and we shall take possession of it. We ask not whether it is valueless or otherwise; be it sterile rock, a barren desert of pathless sand, where no green spot blesses the aching eye, no bubbling fountain cools the parched lips, — *Oregon is ours*, and we will keep it, at the price, if need be, of every drop of the nation's blood.

12. Letter from George D. Phillips to Howell Cobb, dated December

[64] *Niles' National Register*, May 24, 1845, 184.

30, 1845, Clarksville, Georgia:[65]

. . . The President's Message has set all our mountain folks to thinking and talking. Every one understands, or thinks he under stands, all about the Oregon question; and I heard a crowd on Christmas, not one of whom knew on which side of the Rocky Mountains Oregon was, swear they would support and fight for Polk *all over the world*, that he was right, and we would have Oregon and thrash the British into the bargain. . . .

13. Speech by Representative Solomon Foot, Whig from Vermont on February 6, 1846:[66]

Mr. Chairman, when and wherefore all this sudden excitement upon the subject of Oregon? Who are they that have become so clamorous all at once for the whole of Oregon, and who would declare a general war of expulsion from the American continent of every nation who may chance to have a foothold upon any part of it? Who are they that agitate the public mind, and appeal to the popular passions and prejudices; who denounce as treason against our own Government all suggestions of negotiation and compromise, and who would prefer the fearful alternative of war to any treaty arrangement? Who are they that are ever fulminat ing their anathemas against Great Britain, as though they alone were jealous of her power and her designs? Who are they that are ever motivating their oft-repeated professions of sublimated patriotism, as though it were anything more than the frothy decla mation of full-grown demagogism, which evaporates with the

[65] American Historical Association, *Annual Report*, 1911, II, 70 (Washing ton, 1913). (George D. Phillips to Cobb, Dec. 30, 1845.) Ulrich B. Phillips ed., *The Correspondence of Robert Toombs, Alexander H. Stephens, and Howell Cobb*.

[66] *Congressional Globe*, 29th Cong., 1st Sess., Appendix, 251.

breath that utters it? Who are they that arrogate to themselves the privilege of denouncing the conduct and impugning the motives of the advocates of negotiation and compromise, and who denounce as enemies of their own country, and the allies of a foreign Power, those who would avoid the issue of war, and who would maintain the peace which now blesses our land and the world, by all means and measures consistent with the integrity and the honor of the country? Whence comes, I ask, all this sudden storm of patriotic fury, of vaunting arrogance, of vindictive denunciation, of empty and senseless gasconade? Not, I undertake to say, from the industrious, sober, and reflecting portion of the American people, nor yet, indeed, from the best friends and truest patriots of the country. Divest this subject of all extraneous and improper influences; remove from it the instigations and influences of selfish and designing men, of a corrupt and hireling press; remove the instigations and influences of jobbers in stocks and jobbers in politics; remove the instigations and influences of aspiring demagogues, of cuckoo patriots and Tom Thumb heroes; of President-makers and of embryo Presidential candidates; of those who would raise the whirlwind that they might ride upon the storm; of those who would fire the city that they might revel in the plunder of its ruins. Do this, and your Oregon controversy might be settled, peaceably, honorably, and forever, in less than ninety days.

14. Argument of Representative William L. Yancey, Democrat from Alabama, who had supported the annexation of Texas and was later to advocate war with the North, January 7, 1846:[67]

We are on the point, too, of purchasing the magnificent territory of California, which, with Oregon, would give us a breath of

[67] *Congressional Globe*, 29th Cong., 1st Sess., Appendix, 87.

Pacific coast suited to the grandeur and commercial importance of our Republic.

All this would be blighted *by war.* California would be lost to us. A debt of five hundred millions would be imposed upon the country. The paper system, in its worst form, will necessarily have been imposed upon us. The pension list — that spring of life and immortality to patriotic valor — would be almost indefinitely increased. The Government will have become *centralized;* its checks weakened; its administration federalized in all its tendencies. The fabric of State rights will have been swept away, and remain only as a glorious dream; and a strong military bias will have been given to the future career of our country, which, while it may be splendid in appearance, will bear within itself the certain elements of destruction.

15. Speech by Representative Isaac E. Holmes, Democrat from South Carolina, on January 29, 1846:[68]

And here I desire to make an assertion which I do not believe that any military man who has a reputation to lose will deny. I do not believe that any military officer of character will say that we, by means of an army, can take Oregon from the British. I tell you what you can do: you can expel the Hudson Bay Company, if Britain comes not to their assistance. But I put the question again and again: "Can you take Oregon?" There are gentlemen here who, after having made very warlike speeches, admit privately that you cannot take Oregon. How, then, will the second proposition find its consummation; that is to say, the enlargement of the area of freedom? You cannot get the territory; and, therefore, you cannot extend your institutions over it. We are, then, involved in this absurdity: that we go to war for an unattainable

[68] *Congressional Globe,* 29th Cong., 1st Sess., Appendix, 167.

end. Are you not making the experiment of extending freedom by the destruction of all that makes freedom a blessing, which leaves to the individual the right of his own pursuit, and the indulgence, under salutary regulations, of his own will — of remaining where interest invites or duty calls? Are you not, by the very process of war, about to circumscribe the energies of that will, and restrict to the will of another the ideas of propriety or duty? To exchange the broad area of this free country for the limits of a camp, or the circumscriptions of a besieged town? To prevent the intercourse of families, the social indulgencies of friends, the investments of property, and the regulation of one's own concerns? In one word, are you not about to subject the movements of the many to the stern orders of the few? And when, after the lapse of many years, with the loss of thousands of your most gallant sons, amidst the bereavement of widows and the orphanage of the rising generation, you shall have returned to peace, with your industry disordered, with your credit impaired, with your soldiery unpaid, with the habits of men entirely changed, think ye that all will at once settle down into the well-adjusted balances of industrial pursuits? May it not happen that, when the soldiers shall have marched to this capital to demand their pay, a Washington, or the spirit of a Washington, shall be wanted to check the ardor of those demands? And may it not happen that some more aspiring genius, willing to exchange the sword for the sceptre, shall find in this very soldiery the materials with which to erect his throne of empire on the prostrate liberties of the land? We cannot be expected always to be exempt from the vicissitudes of nations. Thus far success has crowned our efforts to establish and extend the benefits of freedom; but success is often the rod which God places in the hands of a presumptuous nation wherewith to chastise itself.

16. Speech by Representative Charles Goodyear, Democrat from New York, on January 16, 1846:[69]

Besides, sir, I said there were mighty interests awaiting the issue. The progress of events, within the few past years has vastly enhanced the value of this territory. When the convention [of 1818] was first entered into, the disputed domain was deemed of little moment; it has even been questioned whether it would not more properly constitute an independent sovereignty than a part of our confederacy. But recent improvements in the facilities of transportation and intercourse have rendered the ports on the Pacific coast contiguous to our territory of immense importance. It can no longer be doubted that, unless the onward progress of our country is checked by a devastating war with Europe, the mouths of the Hudson and the Columbia will, ere long, by means of the railroad and magnetic wires, be brought into close communion. However stupendous the project may appear, its early accomplishment is nevertheless within the limits of the enterprise and highly stimulated energies of the day. The late revolution in the foreign policy of China has awakened the attention of the public to the importance of this overland communication between our Pacific and Atlantic coasts. I can conceive that the whole trade of the Celestial Empire may be diverted through this channel, and that Europe may find her India market where she now purchases her cotton, tobacco, and corn.

But the first step in the prosecution of this vast enterprise cannot be taken until this convention for a joint occupancy is abrogated. Again, sir, our citizens are flowing into that territory in one continuous tide of emigration. They leave behind them the graves of their ancestors, but carry with them, together with our language, our manners and customs, and all those natural affec-

[69] *Ibid.*, 109, 110.

tions which attach them to the land of their birth. They demand the protection of our laws; but this we cannot grant them during the existence of the treaty for joint occupancy. Perfect protection to the citizen admits of no divided sovereignty. And yet we cannot deny it to them, without being recreant to our duty and faithless to our trust. . . .

I am aware, sir, that a claim in our favor paramount to all others has been set up — that of manifest destiny. It runs thus: God hath given to this nation the western continent and the fulness thereof. This, as I understand it, overrides all titles, and sets at defiance all reasoning. This claim to universal dominion was put forth in the commencement of this debate, and has been frequently urged in the course of it; and more particularly by the gentleman from Michigan, [Mr. Chipman,] as a final and conclusive argument. I regretted to hear the sentiment avowed in an American Congress, because it implies a doubt of the validity of our own perfect title, and because it has ever been used to justify every act of wholesale violence and rapine that ever disgraced the history of the world. It is the robber's title; but its record is accompanied by the instructive lesson that it ultimately meets the robber's doom. . . .

17. Speech by Representative Robert Clarke Winthrop, Whig from Massachusetts, on January 3, 1846. Note the rebuttal by Representative William Sawyer (Reading 10):[70]

. . . Of what is the title [to Oregon] made up? . . . I declare to you, sir that as often as I thread the mazes of this controversy, it seems to me to be a dispute as to the relative rights of two parties to a territory, to which neither of them has any real right whatever; and I should hardly blame the other nations of the world for insisting on coming in for scot and lot in the partition of it.

[70] *Ibid.*, 99–100.

Certainly, if we should be so false to our character as civilized nations as to fight about it, the rest of Christendom would be justified, if they had the power, in treating us as we have always treated the savage tribes of our own continent, and turning us both out altogether.

There is one element in our title, however, which I confess that I have not named, and to which I may not have done entire justice. I mean that new revelation of right which has been designated as *the right of our manifest destiny to spread over this whole continent.* It has been openly avowed in a leading Administration journal that this, after all, is our best and strongest title — one so clear, so preeminent, and so indisputable, that if Great Britain had all our other titles in addition to her own, they would weigh nothing against it. The right of our manifest destiny! There is a right for a new chapter in the law of our nations; or rather, in the special laws of our own country; for I suppose the right of a manifest destiny to spread will not be admitted to exist in any nation except the universal Yankee nation! This right of our manifest destiny, Mr. Speaker, reminds me of another source of title, which is worthy of being placed beside it. Spain and Portugal, we all know, in the early part of the sixteenth century, laid claim to the jurisdiction of this whole northern continent of America. Francis I. is said to have replied to this pretension, that he should like to see the clause in *Adam's Will* in which their exclusive title was found. Now, sir, I look for an early reproduction of this idea. I have no doubt that, if due search be made, a copy of this primeval instrument, with a clause giving us the whole of Oregon, can be somewhere hunted up. Perhaps it may be found in that same Illinois cave in which the Mormon Testament has been discovered. I commend the subject to the attention of those in that neighborhood, and will promise to withdraw all my opposition to giving notice or taking possession, whenever the right of our manifest destiny can be fortified by the provisions of our great first parent's will!

18. Speech by Representative Joshua F. Bell, Whig from Kentucky, on February 4, 1846:[71]

It is a useless consumption of time, at this late day of the debate, to detain the committee with a discussion of the title to Oregon. Various sources of title are supposed to exist, but I will not go into them; I will not go into a technical construction of treaties between Spain and England to ascertain their actual or legal meaning; nor into the grant by the "British kings to the early and adventurous colonists, which gave the right to conquer and colonize from sea to sea;" nor examine the claim from continuity and contiguity of territory; nor of the claim resulting from the genius and spirit of our people, and the eternal laws of nature; nor from "the manifest destiny of the republic;" nor from our power to whip England, and, by force of our own swords, take and maintain Oregon.

All these have been relied on with great earnestness and confidence; but most of them are so indefinite, that the time may yet come when our claim may settle down on the two last named, Destiny and Power, and they become important links in the strong chain which binds Oregon to us. For the history of the world, from the earliest establishment of empires among men, proves, that when contiguous territory is necessary to the general, political, or commercial welfare of a particular people, and they have the power to take and keep it, its acquisition becomes a matter of "manifest destiny;" it is not always right, for it is sometimes the "manifest destiny" of nations to do wrong.

[71] *Ibid.*, 210.

III

THE MEXICAN WAR—HOW DOES IT RELATE?

With the annexation of Texas to the Union accomplished, Mexico still refused to honor the Texan claim of independence. In November, 1845, President Polk sent John Slidell to Mexico with offers to settle the Texas boundary controversy with that country and to purchase New Mexico and California. Mexico claimed jurisdiction in all of Texas, but regarded the boundary of the alleged Mexican state of Texas as the Nueces River.

Because of anti-American sentiment in Mexico, that government refused to officially receive or talk with Slidell. Polk then sent troops under the command of General Zachary Taylor (later President from 1849 to 1850) to the Río Bravo del Norte (Rio Grande). In his message to Congress in May, 1846, Polk announced that on April 24 hostilities occurred between Mexican and American troops on the Texas-Mexican border. On May 12, 1846, Congress declared war on Mexico.

In the meantime John C. Frémont, later called the Pathfinder of the West and the man who had mapped out the Oregon Trail, was already in Oregon. He learned of the trouble between Americans and Mexicans in the Sacramento valley in California and, with his troops, went to California and helped to defeat the Mexican forces there.

Of the major battles of the Mexican War there were two main

routes. First, General Taylor defeated the Mexican forces along a route from Palo Alto to Monterrey and then on to Buena Vista (May, 1846, to February, 1847). General Winfield Scott defeated the Mexicans from Vera Cruz to Mexico City (March, 1847, to September, 1847).

Conclusion of the war in 1848 occurred with the Treaty of Guadalupe Hidalgo.

This section is divided into two parts; the first deals with the presidential perspective and support. The second covers opposition to the war.

As you read these parts, ask yourself: Did we get into the war because of Manifest Destiny or because of the failure of diplomacy?

A. The Presidential Perspective and Support

1. President Polk, in his inaugural address on March 4, 1845, stated:[1]

I regard the question of annexation as belonging exclusively to the United States and Texas. They are independent powers competent to contract, and foreign nations have no right to interfere with them or to take exceptions to their reunion. Foreign powers do not seem to appreciate the true character of our Government. Our Union is a confederation of independent States, whose policy is peace with each other and all the world. To enlarge its limits is to extend the dominions of peace over additional territories and increasing millions. The world has nothing to fear from military

---

[1] Inaugural Address of James K. Polk, March 4, 1845. *Inaugural Addresses of the Presidents of the United States from George Washington, 1789, to John F. Kennedy, 1961,* 87th Cong., 1st Sess., House Document No. 218, 96–97.

ambition in our Government. While the Chief Magistrate and the popular branch of Congress are elected for short terms by the suffrages of those millions who must in their own persons bear all the burdens and miseries of war, our Government can not be otherwise than pacific. Foreign powers should therefore look on the annexation of Texas to the United States not as the conquest of a nation seeking to extend her dominions by arms and violence, but as the peaceful acquisition of a territory once her own, by adding another member to our confederation, with the consent of that member, thereby diminishing the chances of war and opening to them new and ever-increasing markets for their products.

To Texas the reunion is important, because the strong protecting arm of our Government would be extended over her, and the vast resources of her fertile soil and genial climate would be speedily developed, while the safety of New Orleans and of our whole southwestern frontier against hostile aggression, as well as the interests of the whole Union, would be promoted by it. . . .

. . . As our population has expanded, the Union has been cemented and strengthened. As our boundaries have been enlarged and our agricultural population has been spread over a large surface, our federative system has acquired additional strength and security. It may well be doubted whether it would not be in greater danger of overthrow if our present population were confined to the comparatively narrow limits of the original thirteen States than it is now that they are sparsely settled over a more expanded territory. It is confidently believed that our system may be safely extended to the utmost bounds of our territorial limits, and that as it shall be extended the bonds of our Union, so far from being weakened, will become stronger.

None can fail to see the danger to our safety and future peace if Texas remains an independent state or becomes an ally or dependency of some foreign nation more powerful than herself. . . .

2. In a message to the Senate dated December 2, 1845, President Polk declared:[2]

If we consider the extent of territory involved in the annexation [of Texas] — its prospective influence on America — the means by which it has been accomplished, springing purely from the choice of the people themselves to share the blessings of our union, — the history of the world may be challenged to furnish a parallel. . . . Our army was ordered to take position in the country between the Nueces and the Del Norte, and to repel any invasion of the Texian territory, which might be attempted by the Mexican forces. Our squadron in the gulf was ordered to co-operate with the army. But though our army and navy were placed in a position to defend our own, and the rights of Texas, they were ordered to commit no act of hostility against Mexico, unless she declared war, or was herself the aggressor by striking the first blow. The result has been, that Mexico has made no aggressive movement, and our military and naval commanders have executed their orders with such discretion that the peace of the two republics has not been disturbed.

3. Waddy Thompson, American representative in Mexico, realized the tremendous value of California and was to a great extent responsible for acquisition of that state. On April 29, 1842, he wrote Daniel Webster:[3]

I believe that this Government would cede to us Texas and the

[2] Thomas Hart Benton, ed., *Abridgment of the Debates of Congress, from 1789 to 1856*, XV (D. Appleton and Company, New York, 1861), 246, 247.

[3] American Historical Association, *Annual Report*, 1914, I (Washington, 1916), 287.

Californias. . . . As to Texas, I regard it as of but little value compared with California — the richest, the most beautiful, the healthiest country in the world. Our Atlantic border secures us a commercial ascendency there; with the acquisition of Upper California we should have the same ascendency on the Pacific. The harbor of St. Francisco is capacious enough to receive the navies of all the world, and the neighborhood furnishes live oak enough to build all the ships of those navies. Besides this there is the Bay of St. Iajo [San Diego], Monterey, and others. . . . The possession of these harbors would . . . no doubt, by internal communication with the Arkansas and other western streams, secure the trade of India and the whole Pacific Ocean.

4. Sam Houston on August 6, 1844, wrote General Zachary Taylor:[4]

I regret that, if emergency should require action, the troops under your command should be compelled to await orders from Washington. I did not so apprehend the regulation when a copy of the treaty was sent to me. Should disaster befall the country, I shall not fail to satisfy myself in the assurance that I did not misapprehend the pledge of the government of the United States, that the President of Texas should at any time command the aid of the military and naval force of the United States in the Gulf and upon the frontiers. This was expected to be done without the delay of an appeal to the government at Washington. I hope all will be well. Be pleased to write to me by express.

5. James Buchanan on October 17, 1845, wrote to Thomas O.

[4] Amelia W. Williams and Eugene C. Barber, eds., *The Writings of Sam Houston, 1821–1847*, IV (The University of Texas Press, Austin, Texas, 1941), 357–358.

Larkin, Consul of the United States at Monterrey:[5]

. . . The interests of our commerce and our whale fisheries on the Pacific ocean demand that you should exert the greatest vigilance in discovering and defeating any attempts which may be made by foreign governments to acquire a control over that country. In the contest between Mexico and California we can take no part, unless the former should commence hostilities against the United States; but should California assert and maintain her independence, we shall render her all the kind offices in our power, as a sister Republic. This Government has no ambitious aspirations to gratify and no desire to extend our federal system over more territory than we already possess, unless by the free and spontaneous wish of the independent people of adjoining territories. The exercise of compulsion or improper influence to accomplish such a result, would be repugnant both to the policy and principles of this Government. But whilst these are the sentiments of the President, he could not view with indifference the transfer of California to Great Britain or any other European Power. The system of colonization by foreign monarchies on the North American continent must and will be resisted by the United States. It could result in nothing but evil to the colonists under their dominion who would naturally desire to secure for themselves the blessings of liberty by means of republican institutions; whilst it must prove highly prejudicial to the best interests of the United States. Nor would it in the end benefit such foreign monarchies. On the contrary, even Great Britain, by the acquisition of California, would sow the seeds of future war and disaster for herself; because there is no political truth more certain than that

[5] John Bassett Moore, ed., *The Works of James Buchanan: Comprising His Speeches, State Papers, and Private Correspondence*, VI (J. B. Lippincott Company, Philadelphia, 1909), 275–276.

this fine Province could not long be held in vassalage by any European Power. The emigration to it of people from the United States would soon render this impossible.

6. President Polk's war message of May 11, 1846:[6]

The [American] army moved from Corpus Christi on the 11th of March, and on the 28th of that month arrived on the left bank of the Del Norte, opposite to Matamoros, where it encamped on a commanding position, which has since been strengthened by the erection of field works. A depot has also been established at Point Isabel, near the Brazos Santiago, thirty miles in rear of the encampment. The selection of his position was necessarily confined to the judgment of the general in command.

The Mexican forces at Matamoros assumed a belligerent attitude, and on the 12th of April, General Ampudia, then in command, notified General Taylor to break up his camp, within twenty-four hours, and to retire beyond the Nueces River; and in the event of his failure to comply with these demands, announced that arms, and arms alone, must decide the question. But no open act of hostility was committed until the 24th of April. On that day, General Arista, who had succeeded to the command of the Mexican forces, communicated to General Taylor that "he considered hostilities commenced, and should prosecute them." A party of dragoons of sixty-three men and officers were on the same day despatched from the American camp up the Rio del Norte, on its left bank, to ascertain whether the Mexican troops had crossed, or were preparing to cross, the river "became engaged with a large body of these troops, and after a short affair, in which some sixteen were killed and wounded, appear to have been surrounded and compelled to surrender."

[6] Thomas Hart Benton, ed., *Abridgement of the Debates of Congress, from 1789 to 1856*, XV (D. Appleton and Company, New York, 1861), 486.

7. Thomas Hart Benton recalled activities in California:[7]

. . . Mr. Frémont was pursuing science and shunning war, when the arrival of Lieutenant Gillispie, and his communications from Washington, suddenly changed all his plans, turned him back from Oregon, and opened a new and splendid field of operations in California itself. He arrived in the valley of the Sacramento in the month of May, 1846, and found the country alarmingly, and critically situated. Three great operations, fatal to American interests, were then going on, and without remedy, if not arrested at once. These were: 1. The massacre of the Americans, and the destruction of their settlements in the valley of the Sacramento. 2. The subjection of California to British protection. 3. The transfer of the public domain to British subjects, and all this with a view to anticipate the events of a Mexican war, and to shelter California from the arms of the United States.

The American settlers sent a deputation to the camp of Mr. Frémont, in the valley of the Sacramento, laid all these dangers before him, and implored him to place himself at their head and save them from destruction. General Castro [of the Mexican Army in California] was then in march upon them: the Indians were incited to attack their families, and burn their wheat fields, and were only waiting for the dry season to apply the torch. Juntas were in session to transfer the country to Great Britain: the public domain was passing away in large grants to British subjects: a British fleet was expected on the coast: the British vice-consul, Forbes, and the emissary priest, Macnamara, ruling and conducting every thing: and all their plans so far advanced as to render the least delay fatal. It was then the beginning of June. War had broken out between the United States and Mexico,

[7] Thomas Hart Benton, *Thirty Years' View,* II (D. Appleton and Company, New York, 1854), 691.

but that was unknown in California. Mr. Frémont had left the two countries at peace when he set out upon his expedition, and was determined to do nothing to disturb their relations: he had even left California to avoid giving offence; and to return and take up arms in so short a time was apparently to discredit his own previous conduct as well as to implicate his government. He felt all the responsibilities of his position; but the actual approach of Castro, and the immediate danger of the settlers, left him no alternative. He determined to put himself at the head of the people, and to save the country. To repulse Castro was not sufficient; to overturn the Mexican government in California, and to establish Californian Independence, was the bold resolve, and the only measure adequate to the emergency. That resolve was taken, and executed with a celerity that gave it a romantic success. The American settlers rushed to his camp — brought their arms, horses and ammunition — were formed into a battalion; and obeyed with zeal and alacrity the orders they received. In thirty days all the northern part of California was freed from Mexican authority — Independence proclaimed — Castro flying to the south — the American settlers saved from destruction; and the British party in California counteracted and broken up in all their schemes.

This movement for Independence was the salvation of California, and snatched it out of the hands of the British at the moment they were ready to clutch it.

8. Polk recorded in his diary on October 24, 1845:[8]

The conversation then turned on California, on which I remarked that Great Britain had her eye on that country and

[8] M. M. Quaife, ed., *The Diary of James K. Polk During His Presidency, 1845 to 1849* (A. C. McClurg and Co., Chicago, 1910), 71.

intended to possess it if she could, but that the people of the U. S. would not willingly permit California to pass into the possession of any new colony planted by Great Britain or any foreign monarchy, and that in reasserting Mr. Monroe's doctrine, I had California & the fine bay of San Francisco as much in view as Oregon. Col. [Thomas Hart] Benton agreed that no Foreign Power ought to be permitted to colonize California, any more than they would be to colonize Cuba. As long as Cuba remained in the possession of the present Government we would not object, but if a powerful foreign power was about to possess it, we would not permit it. On the same footing we would place California.

9. Polk's diary of April 22, 1846:[9]

The truth is that in all this Oregon discussion in the Senate, too many Democratic Senators have been more concerned about the Presidential election in '48, than they have been about settling Oregon either at 49° or 54° 40'. "Forty-eight" has been with them the Great question, and hence the divisions in the Democratic party. I cannot but observe the fact, and for the sake of the country I deeply deplore it. I will however do my duty whatever may happen. I will rise above the interested factions in Congress, and appeal confidently to the people for support.

10. Polk's diary of May 9, 1846:[10]

The Cabinet held a regular meeting today; all the members present. I brought up the Mexican question, and the question of what was the duty of the administration in the present state of our relations with that country. The subject was very fully dis-

[9] *Ibid.*, 345.
[10] *Ibid.*, 384–385.

cussed. All agreed that if the Mexican forces at Matamoros committed any act of hostility on Gen'l Taylor's forces I should immediately send a message to Congress recommending an immediate declaration of War. I stated to the Cabinet that up to this time, as they knew, we had heard of no open act of aggression by the Mexican army, but that the danger was imminent that such acts would be committed. I said that in my opinion we had ample cause of war, and that it was impossible that we could stand in *statu quo*, or that I could remain silent much longer; that I thought it was my duty to send a message to Congress very soon & recommend definitive measures. I told them that I thought I ought to make such a message by tuesday next, that the country was excited and impatient on the subject, and if I failed to do so I would not be doing my duty. I then propounded the distinct question to the Cabinet and took their opinions individually, whether I should make a message to Congress on tuesday, and whether in that message I should recommend a declaration of War against Mexico. All except the Secretary of the Navy gave their advice in the affirmative. Mr. Bancroft dissented but said if any act of hostility should be committed by the Mexican forces he was then in favour of immediate war. Mr. Buchanan said he would feel better satisfied in his course if the Mexican forces had or should commit any act of hostility, but that as matters stood we had ample cause of war against Mexico, & he gave his assent to the measure.

11. During this period, the Reverend Walter Colton recalled activities in California:[11]

Wednesday, Sept. 16 [1846]

Gen. Castro had taken up his position just outside the Pueblo,

[11] Rev. Walter Colton, *Three Years in California* (A. S. Barnes and Co., New York, 1851), 56, 72–73, 88.

on an elevation which commands the town and adjacent country. He was well supplied with field-pieces, and had a force of seven hundred men. Com. Stockton landed at San Pedro with three hundred seamen and marines from the Congress, and marched against him. His route, which extended some thirty miles, lay through several narrow passes, which Gen. Castro might easily have defended against a much superior force. But the general kept in his entrenched camp; and informed the commodore by a courier, that if he marched upon the town he would find it the grave of his men. "Then," said the commodore, "tell the general to have the bells ready to toll in the morning at eight o'clock, as I shall be there at that time." He was there; but Castro, in the meantime, had broken up his camp, mounted with an armed band, and fled towards Sonora, in Mexico. The town was taken, the American flag hoisted and cheered.

* * * * * *

Tuesday, Oct. 13 [1846]

Emigrants from the United States are still pouring into the rich valley of the Sacramento. A letter from one of them says: — "It may not be uninteresting to you to know that the emigrants by land the present season far exceed the expectation of the most sanguine. No less than two thousand are now in the interior, and within a hundred miles of the settlements. They bring with them a large amount of intelligence, wealth, and industry, all of which are greatly needed in their new home. The Mormons alone have a train of more than three hundred wagons."

These emigrants will change the face of California. We shall soon have not only the fruits of nature, but of human industry. We shall soon be able to get a ball of butter without churning it on the back of a wild colt; and a potatoe without weighing it as if it were a doubloon. Were it possible for a man to live without the trouble of drawing his breath, I should look for this pleasing phenomenon in California.

* * * * * *

Sunday, Nov. 8 [1846]

There is not, except myself, a Protestant clergyman in California. If the tide of emigration continues, there will be thousands here without a spiritual teacher. Years must elapse before any can be trained here for the sacred office. The supply must come from abroad. The American churches must wake up to their duty on this subject. These emigrants are their children, and they should extend to them their most jealous care.

12. Polk's diary of November 20, 1847:[12]

. . . The Cabinet all agreed that there should be a paragraph to the effect that the citizens of Mexico in favour of peace should be protected by our army in establishing a Government able and willing to make a just peace, but, if we failed to obtain a peace by this means, the question was what I should state would be our policy. In Mr. Buchanan's draft he stated in that event that "we must fulfil that destiny which Providence may have in store for both countries." I thought this would be too indefinite & that it would be avoiding my constitutional responsibility. I preferred to state in substance that we should, in that event, take the measure of our indemnity into our own hands, and dictate our own terms to Mexico. . . .

13. At the onset of war, General Taylor sent the Mexican people a

[12] M. M. Quaife, ed., *The Diary of James K. Polk During His Presidency, 1845 to 1849*, III (A. C. McClurg and Co., Chicago, 1910), 226.

proclamation. (Translated from the Spanish.)[13]

To the people of Mexico:

. . . Your Government is in the hands of tyrants and usurpers. They have abolished your State governments, they have overthrown your federal constitution, they have deprived you of the right of suffrage, destroyed the liberty of the press, despoiled you of your arms, and reduced you to a state of absolute dependence upon the power of a military dictator. Your army and rulers extort from the people by grievous taxation, by forced loans, and military seizures the very money which sustains the usurpers in power. Being disarmed, you are left defenseless, an easy prey to the savage Comanches, who not only destroy your lives and property, but drive into a captivity, more horrible than death itself, your wives and children. It is your military rulers who have reduced you to this deplorable condition. It is these tyrants and their corrupt and cruel satellites, gorged with the people's treasures, by whom you are thus oppressed and impoverished, some of whom have boldly advocated a monarchial government, and would place a European prince on the throne of Mexico. We come to obtain indemnity for the past and security for the future, we come to overthrow the tyrants who have destroyed your liberties; but we come to make no war upon the people of Mexico, nor upon any form of free government they may choose to select for themselves. . . . It is the settled policy of your tyrants to deceive you in regard to the policy and character of our Government and people. These tyrants fear the example of our free institutions, and constantly endeavor to misrepresent our purposes and inspire you with hatred for your republican brethren of the American Union. Give us but the opportunity to undeceive you

[13] *Senate Document* 896, 62nd Cong., 2d Sess., December 4, 1911–August 26, 1912, Vol. 40 (Washington, 1912), 19–20.

and you will soon learn that all the representatives of Paredes were false, and were only made to induce you to consent to the establishment of a despotic government.

14. Speech by Senator Sidney Breese, Democrat from Illinois, on February 23, 1847.[14]

But, sir, the war is not the act of the Executive. Why, I would ask, should the President desire a war with Mexico, or with any other Power? (*Cui bono?*) How is he to be benefited by it? What personal gratification can it be to him to see his country involved in a war? No, sir; it is the act of Mexico alone, and placed by her, not on the ground Senators have assumed — the movement of the army of occupation to the Rio Grande, by the order of the President — but upon her avowed determination to *recover* Texas, if the measure of annexation was consummated. . . .

With full knowledge of the declarations of Mexico, that she would declare war in the event of annexation, the American people expressed their opinions upon the question, by the election of those candidates who were publicly known to be favorable to the measure — fifteen States giving them their suffrage, against eleven States voting for candidates understood to be opposed to it. No one, I think, Mr. President, will deny that the question of annexation and "the whole of Oregon," were the principle turning points of the election of 1844; that if these issues had not been presented to the country, the successful party would have been in the other predicament. The people, then, decided for annexation at the hazard of war. They believed the measure of sufficient importance to our peace, and safety, and prosperity, to justify the risk. . . .

[14] *Congressional Globe,* 29th Cong., 2d Sess., Appendix, 206–207.

15. Speech by Representative Charles J. Ingersoll, Whig from Pennsylvania, on January 19, 1847:[15]

. . . President Polk's war. I deny it. It is my war, it is your war; it is the war of these United States; all represented in Congress assembled. It is our act — ay, the act of the minority, too, of the fourteen members voting against it, if majorities rule and minorities are bound by law. It is the act, a solemn and signal act, of the whole country. Never was an act more so, passed almost by acclamation, almost unanimously, without hesitation or delay. We pulled the trigger; we applied the match; and it is now impossible to stop the ball but by deserting our guns, and flying from the enemy. There is no other option — no alternative but disgraceful retreat . . .

16. Speech by Senator Sam Houston, Democrat from Texas, on February 19, 1847:[16]

But to return from this digression: [I] could not believe that peace could ever be brought about with Mexico until she had felt the calamities of war. We must march, not merely to her borders to annoy her there — for we should only add to the miseries of her inhabitants and the extortion of her rulers, by affording them a pretence for extortion under the plea of necessity to defend the country — we must strike home. Let them know that we are not warring against the rights of their citizens — against the oppressed people of Mexico, nor their priesthood, nor their religion. Show them that you will respect their temples, treat their images with deference, and, however much you may differ from their religious opinions, teach them that they will be entitled

[15] *Ibid.*, 125.
[16] *Ibid.*, 222.

to freedom of thought, and the most perfect liberty. Show them that you only intend to chastise their tyrants and oppressors. Go to their capital, and we would not doubt of success in this war. If everything has not already been achieved, it is no reason why we should despair of the most perfect success. We *can* conquer Mexico.

17. Speech by Representative Henry Bedinger, Democrat from Virginia, on January 6, 1847:[17]

But we are now asked, for what is this war carried on? What is its object? Is it to be a war of conquest? I answer, with all my heart I do sincerely hope so. I hope it is to be a war of conquest on our part: of one conquest after another, as rapid and brilliant as those which have already astonished the world. I trust in Heaven, in the justice of our cause, and in the bravery of our armies, that it shall be nothing but a war of conquest. It is waged, sir, for the purpose of procuring an honorable peace — for the purpose of revenging the insults and outrages which we have received — for the purpose of avenging the blood of our citizens shed on our own soil — for the purpose of teaching a barbarous people how to regard the laws of nations — for the purpose of teaching demi-savages the rules of civilization, of decency, and common courtesy — for the purpose of letting the world see that we know how to preserve and defend our rights and our sacred honor. And if my wishes could govern the action of this Government, everything should be made to yield to the vigorous prosecution of this war. One blow should follow another in quick and rapid succession, until Mexico chose to come to her senses. Sir,

[17] *Ibid.*, 85.

I am not one of those who, having entered into a fight, dislike to strike hard blows. I would show no mercy, sir — no mercy, until reparation were made for the wrongs we have endured, and the blood and treasure we have spent. I would heed no idle clamors, whether proceeding from the envy of foreign Powers, or the pretended patriotism of domestic opponents. Sir, would gentlemen have this to be a war of defeats on our part, that they are so clamorous against a "war of conquest"? Would they see our armies driven in disgrace from Mexico, and her flag floating in triumph upon the banks of the Rio Bravo? I hope not, sir. I repeat again that I hope this war may be prosecuted with vigor to conquest and to victory; and I believe it will be so prosecuted; I rely upon the bravery of our armies, and the patriotism of the American people, to see it speedily terminated, covering our national character with glory and honor.

18. Speech by Senator John C. Calhoun of South Carolina, on March 16, 1846:[18]

I am, finally, opposed to war, because peace — peace is preeminently our policy. There may be nations, restricted small territories, hemmed in on all sides, so situated that war may be necessary to their greatness. Such is not our case. Providence has given us an inheritance stretching across the entire continent from East to West, from ocean to ocean, and from North to South, covering by far the greater and better part of its temperate zone. It comprises a region not only of vast extent, but abundant in all resources; excellent in climate; fertile and exuberant in soil; capable of sustaining in the plentiful enjoyment of all the necessaries of life a population of ten times our present number. Our

18 *Congressional Globe*, 29th Cong., 1st Sess., Appendix, 475.

great mission, as a people, is to occupy this vast domain; to replenish it with an intelligent, virtuous, and industrious population; to convert the forests into cultivated fields; to drain the swamps and morasses, and cover them with rich harvests, to build up cities, towns, and villages in every direction, and to unite the whole by the most rapid intercourse between all the parts. War would but impede the fulfilment of this high mission, by absorbing the means and diverting the energies which would be devoted to the purpose. . . .

19. Speech by Senator Calhoun on February 9, 1847:[19]

. . . It is a remarkable fact in the history of this continent, that the aborigines in this and the adjacent portions of Mexico, encroach upon the European occupants. The Indians are actually gaining ground upon the Mexicans; not but that they are brave and capable of defending themselves with arms, but the jealousy of the Central Government had in a great measure disarmed them, while, from its feebleness and remoteness, it is incapable of affording them protection. It is said that there are not less than three or four thousand captives from New Mexico and the neighboring States, in the hands of the Indians. Such being the state of things, it is manifest that while the acquisition would be of great importance to us, it would, instead of being a loss to the Mexicans, be a positive gain. The possession by our people would protect the whole of the adjacent portions of Mexico from the incursions and ravages of the Indians, and give it a greater degree of security and prosperity than it ever has experienced from the commencement of her revolution, now more than a quarter of a century ago.

[19] *Congressional Globe*, 29th Cong., 2nd Sess., Appendix, 325.

The next consideration is, that the line should be such, if it should be established as a boundary, as would lay the foundation of a permanent peace between us and Mexico; and here again it has remarkable advantages; it is impossible for us to prevent our growing population from passing into an uninhabited country, where the power of the owners is not sufficient to keep them out. In they will go. We may pass laws, heaping penalty upon penalty; but they will be of no avail to prevent our pioneers from forcing themselves into the country, unless efficiently resisted by the Power in possession. Of this we have abundant proof from experience in our relations with the Indians. Many and severe laws have been passed to prevent intrusion upon them, with little effect. In the end, the only remedy has been found to be, to purchase their lands, and remove them to a greater distance. If such is the case with the Indians, where the population is more dense, and our means of preventing intrusion much greater, it would be vain to expect that we could prevent our people from penetrating into California, or that the Government of Mexico would be able to prevent their doing so. Even before our present difficulties with Mexico, the process had begun. Under such circumstances, to make peace with Mexico without acquiring a considerable portion, at least of this uninhabited region, would lay the foundation of new troubles, and subject us to the hazard of further conflicts — a result equally undesirable to Mexico and ourselves. But it is not only in reference to a permanent peace with Mexico that it is desirable that this vast uninhabited region should pass into our possession. High considerations connected with civilization and commerce make it no less so. We alone can people it with an industrious and civilized race, which can develope [sic] its resources and add a new and extensive region to the domain of commerce and civilization. Left as it is, it must remain for generations an uninhabited and barren waste.

20. Speech by Senator Lewis Cass, Democrat from Michigan. Cass had fought against Tecumseh, was Governor of the Michigan Territory, Jackson's Secretary of War, Minister Plenipotentiary to France, and Buchanan's Secretary of State. On February 10, 1847, Cass made this speech in his defense of the Mexican War:[20]

In Europe one of the social evils is concentration. Men are brought too much and kept too much in contact. There is not room for expansion. Minds of the highest order are pressed down by adverse circumstances, without the power of free exertion. There is no starting-point for them. Hence the struggles, that are ever going on, in our crowded communities. And hence the *émeutes*, which disturb and alarm the Governments of the Old World, and which must one day or other shake them to their centre. Questions of existence are involved in them, as well as questions of freedom. I trust we are far removed from all this; but to remove us further yet, we want almost unlimited power of expansion. That is our safety valve. . . .

21. Speech by Senator H. V. Johnson, Whig from Louisiana, during debates over the Mexican War:[21]

In the progress of the discussions on the topics connected with the war, a good deal has been said in ridicule, of what is called, "manifest destiny." Now, sir, I am a believer in this doctrine; but

[20] *Ibid.*, 189.
[21] *Congressional Globe*, 30th Cong., 1st Sess., Appendix, 379–380.

I would not employ precisely these words to express my opinion. I would say, that I believe it to be the manifest design of Providence, either that the whole of North America should be embraced within our Republic, or that, through the influence of our institutions, it is to become the theatre of the highest civilization and freedom. Yet, sir, I am no propagandist. I would not force the adoption of our form of Government upon any people, by the sword. But if war is forced upon us, as this has been, and the increase of our territory, and consequently the extension of the area of human liberty and happiness, shall be one of the incidents of such a contest, I believe we should be recreant to our noble mission, if we refused acquiescence in the high purposes of a wise Providence. War has its evils. In all ages it has been the minister of wholesale death and appalling desolation; but however inscrutable to us, it has also been made, by the All-wise Dispenser of events, that instrumentality of accomplishing the great end of human elevation and human happiness. Civilization, like her heaven-born pioneer mother, Christianity, has been compelled to force on her steady march, for more than eighteen hundred years, amidst the revolutions of empires, which have stained with blood her robe of whiteness. But, converting every obstacle to her progress into a weapon of victory, she shall encincture the globe with her girdle of light. It is in this view, that I believe the whole of North America is consecrated to freedom. Neither legislation nor treaties can set bounds to the triumphant spirit of the age, which threatens thrones and dynasties, and augurs an entire remodeling and renovation of the social and political condition of the world. The results of war and the developments of science are but the echoes of the voice of prophecy. The one opens the door for civilization, and the other sends its ministers by the power of steam, and speeds them upon the wing of the "seraphic lightning."

22. Address of Commander R. F. Stockton, December 30, 1847, before a crowd in New York City:[22]

. . . But we have a duty before God which we cannot — we must not evade. The priceless boon of civil and religious liberty has been confided to us as trustees — [cheers] — I would insist, if the war were to be prolonged for fifty years, and cost money enough to demand from us each year the half of all that we possess, I would still insist that the inestimable blessings of civil and religious liberty should be guaranteed to Mexico. We must not shrink from the solemn duty. . . .

23. Statement issued by the New York State Democratic Convention, January 26, 1848:[23]

. . . We (the American people) have devolved upon us the great work of restoring to man his long lost rights. The means by which we are to accomplish this end ought to be legally as well as morally just. The field is in part opened to us by the conduct of Mexico, and such moral and legal means are offered for our use. Shall we occupy it? Shall we now run with manly vigor the race that is set before us? Or shall we yield to the suggestions of a sickly fanaticism, and sink into an enervating slumber? Labor was the consecrated means of man's subsistence when he was created. To replenish the earth and subdue it, was his ordained mission and destiny. . . .

[22] *Niles' National Register*, January 22, 1848, 335.
[23] *Niles' National Register*, February 19, 1848, 391.

B. The Perspective of Opposition

1. A statement of prevailing doctrines, January 22, 1848, as reported by *Niles' National Register*:[24]

"MANIFEST DESTINY" DOCTRINES

Amongst the many journals published in our country, that boldly advocate the doctrine that it is the duty of the people of this country to conquer and retain the Mexican republic, in order to *compel* that people to submit to such institutions as we choose to impose, none is more explicit than the New York *Evening Post*. In an argument upon the subject the editor says:

"Now we ask, whether any man can coolly contemplate the idea of recalling our troops from the territory we at present occupy . . . and thus, by one stroke of a secretary's pen, resign this beautiful country to the custody of the ignorant cowards and profligate ruffians who have ruled it for the last twenty years? Why, humanity cries out against it. Civilization and Christianity protest against this reflux of the tide of barbarism and anarchy."

And again, "the aborigines of this country have not attempted and cannot attempt, to exist *independently* alongside of us. Providence has so ordained it; and it is folly not to recognize the fact. The Mexicans are *aboriginal Indians,* and they must share the destiny of their race."

The "destiny of the race" of "*aboriginal Indians* along side of us" has been *extinction* — rapid extinction — not subjection, as we all know. They never have submitted to become slaves. Is it then seriously contemplated that the seven millions of Mexican Indians *shall not* exist independently along side of us? — and pro-

[24] *Niles' National Register,* January 22, 1848, 334.

nounced to be "a folly not to recognize the fact, that Providence has so ordained it?"

Numerous articles of the same import are gracing journals published in this free, this enlightened, this *Christian* country — *this model republic.*

2. Speech by Representative Luther Severance, Whig from Maine, on February 4, 1847:[25]

Sir, I am one of the fourteen members of the House who, in May last, voted against the bill authorizing the President to call for fifty thousand volunteers, and appropriating ten millions of dollars to prosecute the war with Mexico; and I will here enumerate fourteen reasons why I am still opposed to prosecuting the war, and why I cannot vote further appropriations to carry it on. These reasons are:

1. Because the war was wrongfully and unjustly commenced by the President, while Congress was in session, without asking its consent.

2. Because it is a war of conquest, and was commenced, and is now continued, with that design.

3. Because war did not exist by the act of Mexico, and did not exist legally until Congress recognised it in May last.

4. Because there is no other way in which I can, *by my vote*, manifest my opposition to the continuance of the war.

5. Because, in refusing men and money to prosecute the war in a foreign country, I do not endanger the safety of a single individual, or a single interest, in my own country.

[25] *Congressional Globe,* 29th Cong., 2d Sess., Appendix, 282.

6. Because the war is a prodigal squandering of human life and national treasure, without any benefit to the country or to mankind.

7. Because a war between the two largest republics in the world is not calculated to spread the principles of civil liberty and elective government.

8. Because an acquisition of territory, for the purpose of establishing slavery where it has once been abolished, would be turning backward in the march of civilization, and be a national calamity, even were the acquisition bloodless, honestly obtained, and without cost.

9. Because, even if the territory acquired be made free, aggressive war is not an approved mode of extending the "area of freedom," or of obtaining respect for republican principles.

10. Because I regard as utterly absurd any attempt to force a people into our Union against their consent.

11. Because, if we had their consent, we should be better off without them.

12. Because the money foolishly spent in this war by the two countries would have built a railroad and a line of telegraph to Oregon, and a ship canal across the isthmus.

13. Because all war, but that which is strictly defensive, ought, in this age of the Christian world, to be regarded as criminal and barbarous.

14. Because the triumphs of peace are far more glorious and more enduring than those of the sword.

3. Speech by Charles Hobart Carroll, a Henry Clay Whig and Representative from New York, on February 22, 1847.[26] He also was a presidential elector on the American Party ticket in 1856.

No, sir. This war was made in consequence of the annexation of Texas and the consequent acts of the President. It was in consequence of the President's having ordered forward his army to the Rio Grande, not to protect Texas, as he pretends, but, in a threatening manner, to challenge the Mexican commander to come over and fight. So anxious was the President to get us into this war that he sent our general into the disputed territory, not to protect Texas (for there were none there) but to dare the Mexican general and give him a challenge. Therefore he ordered General Taylor to plant his cannon opposite a Mexican town, and point them so as to threaten it with bombardment.

But the President and his partisans on this floor say that the war was begun by Mexico, because blood was first spilt by the Mexicans. But was this blood shed upon soil recognised by Mexico as belonging to Texas, or upon soil inhabited by Texians? Not at all. The whole population, from Corpus Christi to the Rio Grande was Mexican. There was not a Texian on the Rio Grande. Was it to be wondered at, under all the circumstances, that the Mexicans should be exasperated at seeing the American army erecting batteries and fortifications on soil occupied by Mexican citizens? Could the President of the United States have expected less when he sent his army to the Rio Grande than it would be attacked by the Mexicans? If he did, he calculated on their cowardice, and not on his prudence or desire to preserve the peaceable relations between the two countries.

[26] *Congressional Globe*, 29th Cong., 2d Sess., Appendix, 415.

4. Argument of Representative Garrett Davis, a Henry Clay Whig from Kentucky, on December 22, 1846.[27]

For what did Mr. Polk send General Taylor's army to the Rio Grande, but to conquer and hold the country upon it? What object could he have in giving Colonel Stevenson orders to raise a regiment of men of various pursuits, and such as would be likely to remain at the end of the war, either in Oregon or any other territory in that region of the globe which may then be a part of the United States, with an express stipulation that they were not to be brought home by the Government, but [serve for] conquest, settlement, and occupation? The Mormons had been forcibly broken up and driven from Illinois, and were wandering in search of a new home. Why did the Secretary of War, in his orders to General Kearny, say:

"It is known that a large body of Mormon emigrants are en route to California, for the purpose of settling in that country. You are desired to use all proper means to have a good understanding with them, to the end that the United States may have their cooperation in taking possession of and holding that country."

Why did Mr. Polk receive into the service of the United States a legion of Mormons, five hundred in strength? Why was General Kearny ordered by Mr. Polk *to conquer and take possession of New Mexico and Upper California,* and to establish temporary governments in them? . . .

5. Speech by Representative Joshua R. Giddings, anti-slavery Whig from Ohio, on December 15, 1846:[28]

. . . The President avows his intention to hold the territory

27 *Ibid.,* 110.
28 *Ibid.,* 50.

which we have conquered until Mexico shall repay us this expenditure. We have waged an unnecessary and unjust war upon a weak and defenseless republic. We have squandered untold millions in its prosecution; and now the President expresses his intention to rob Mexico of her territory, unless she repays the money we have so profusely spent. This we all know she can never do. The avowal, therefore, amounts to a declaration of the President's intention to render it a war of conquest. Indeed, we have abundant evidence of such intention.

During the darker ages, and among savage nations, such a war might have been tolerated; but it will surely be condemned by all Christian nations of the nineteenth century. Such a war is opposed to the sentiment of the age in which we live. Sir, I would as soon lend my vote to commence a system of national robbery or piracy, as I would support a war commenced for the evident purpose of wresting from a neighboring Government a portion of her territory. But how much Mexican territory does the President think it will require to indemnify us for our expenditure? How much land will he demand for the two thousand American citizens whose lives have been sacrificed in this war?

6. Speech by Representative Milton Brown, Whig from Tennessee, on February 12, 1847. He was later president of the Mississippi Central and Tennessee and Mobile railroad companies.[29]

Mr. Chairman: Though reluctant to speak at a time when speeches on this floor seem so abundant, a sense of duty compels me to present my views of the causes and origin of this war. That its *immediate* cause and origin are to be found in the marching of our army into the Mexican settlements on the Rio Grande,

[29] *Ibid.*, 354, 357.

and pointing our cannon into the Mexican city of Matamoros, seems too clear to admit of reasonable controversy. The proof of this — *conclusive and unanswerable* — stands in the public documents of the country, now exposed to public inspection, to be seen and read by all.

But the defenders of the President, driven almost to desperation to find apologies for this most unauthorized and unwarrantable act, have attempted to defend it on the ground of its being necessary to carry out the Texas annexation resolution, passed by the Congress of the United States. And, strange to say, my colleagues, [Mr. Martin, Mr. Stanton, and Mr. Johnson,] anxious to shield the President, and at the same time to connect myself, who introduced the annexation resolution which finally proved successful, and other Whigs, who voted for it, with the responsibilities of this war, have assumed that annexation itself rendered a conflict of arms with Mexico inevitable. In doing this, they have been driven to the humiliating necessity of contradicting all that the President himself and his friends have declared to the country, both before and since annexation, even up to the commencement of the war. *Before* the passage of the annexation resolution they declared that annexation would be no cause of offence to Mexico, and that it would produce no war. *After* annexation, it was triumphantly proclaimed that no war had ensued, or was likely to ensue; and Mr. Polk, in his message of December, 1845, announced the consummation of the great event, as "*a bloodless achievement,*" in which the arm of force and sword of war had taken no part.

But there are to my mind other unanswerable difficulties in the way of bringing this territory in, with its Mexican inhabitants. Waiving the question whether these inhabitants are capable of self-government, or can be made so, which is matter of extreme doubt, still other insuperable objections, to my mind, are in the way. The doctrines of our Declaration of Independence, and the spirit and genius of our institutions, recognise but one foundation on which free government can rest, the *"consent of the governed."* To *force* a reluctant people to submit to our institutions, as we must do if we bring this Mexican population under our Constitution, would be contrary to its principles. Texas came in, but she was free, and came in by the consent of her people, deliberately expressed. But suppose Texas while free, from some cause, had waged war against us, and our arms being victorious, we proposed, in order to "indemnify us for the expenses of the war," to annex a part or all of her territory to the United States, notwithstanding the people we proposed to bring in should be unwilling to come under our Federal Constitution, ought we under such circumstances to have forced them in? I think not. It would have been in violation of the spirit of our Government.

7. Speech by Representative Joshua F. Bell, Whig from Kentucky, on January 19, 1847:[30]

. . . The President says that we had two causes of complaint against Mexico; that we had an unsettled boundary between Texas and Mexico, and that our citizens had just claims against Mexico to the amount of five or six millions of dollars; that, to settle these subjects of dispute, he had sent Mr. Slidell as minister plenipotentiary to Mexico, but that the Mexican Government, feeling itself outraged by the annexation of Texas, refused to receive Mr. Slidell as a full minister, offering to receive him as minister to settle the Texas difficulty first, and after that, to adjust the question of money due our citizens. Mr. Slidell was instructed by Mr. Polk to have both questions settled together; and the

[30] *Ibid.,* 249.

Mexican Government was threatened that if both were not at once and together settled, that war would be the consequence. The Mexican Government again refused the union of questions, and again declared its willingness to settle them, taking first the question growing out of the annexation of Texas. Whilst this negotiation was going on, the President, anticipating the rejection of his minister, ordered the army to march up to the Rio Grande, and opposite the Mexican town of Matamoros; and upon his rejection, in fact before it, a conflict between the American and Mexican army took place, and the war begun.

Now, sir, I have stated fairly, but in condensed form, the grounds taken by the President in relation to this war. So it may be clearly seen that, even according to the President's own show-ing, if our President would have consented to settle the question of boundary first — in other words, to call Mr. Slidell a special Minister, rather than Minister Plenipotentiary — we would not have had this war; this effusion of blood and expenditure of money might have been saved. We are fighting, then, on a mere matter of etiquette. Now, sir, when you send men many thousand miles from home, on such perilous enterprises, to shed their blood to settle this question of ceremony, it is right that you should pay them well. I do not believe that Mexico was right in refusing our Minister for the reason stated; on the contrary, she was wrong. Her weakness was her only apology for such a refusal.

8. Abraham Lincoln, then a representative from Illinois, on December 21, 1847, introduced the following resolutions in the House of Representatives.[31]

Whereas the President of the United States, in his message of May 11th. 1846, has declared that "The Mexican Government not

[31] *Congressional Globe*, 30th Cong., 1st Sess., 64.

only refused to receive him, [the envoy of the U.S.] or listen to his propositions, but, after a long continued series of menaces, have at last invaded *our territory* and shed the blood of our fellow *citizens* on *our own soil*":

And again, in his message of December 8, 1846, that "we had ample cause of war against Mexico, long before the breaking out of hostilities; but even then we forbore to take redress into our own hands until Mexico herself became the aggressor, by invading *our soil* in hostile array and shedding the blood of our *citizens*":

And yet again, in his message of December 7, 1847, that "the Mexican Government refused even to hear the terms of adjustment which he [our minister of peace] was authorized to propose, and finally, under wholly unjustifiable pretexts, involved the two countries in war, by invading the territory of the State of Texas, striking the first blow, and shedding the blood of our *citizens* on *our own soil*":

And whereas this House is desirous to obtain a full knowledge of all the facts which go to establish whether the particular spot of soil on which the blood of our citizens was so shed was or was not at that time *our own soil:* Therefore,

Resolved by the House of Representatives, That the President of the United States be respectfully requested to inform this House —

1st. Whether the spot of soil on which the blood of our citizens was shed, as in his messages declared, was, or was not within the territories of Spain, at least from the treaty of 1819 until the Mexican revolution.

2d. Whether that spot is or is not within the territory which was wrested from Spain by the revolutionary Government of Mexico.

3d. Whether that spot is or is not within a settlement of people, which settlement had existed ever since long before the Texas revolution, until its inhabitants fled from the approach of the United States army.

4th. Whether that settlement is or is not isolated from any and all other settlements by the Gulf of Mexico and the Rio Grande on the south and west, and by wide uninhabited regions on the north and east.

5th. Whether the people of that settlement, or a majority of them, or any of them, have ever submitted themselves to the government or laws of Texas or of the United States, by consent or by compulsion, either by accepting office, or voting at elections, or paying taxes, or serving on juries, or having process served upon them, or in any other way.

6th. Whether the people of that settlement did or did not flee from the approach of the United States army, leaving unprotected their homes and their growing crops, *before* the first blood, so shed was, or was not shed within the enclosure of one of the people who had thus fled from it.

7th. Whether our *citizens,* whose blood was shed, as in his messages declared, were or were not, at that time, armed officers and soldiers, sent into that settlement by the military order of the President, through the Secretary of War.

8th. Whether the military force of the United States was, or was not so sent into that settlement after General Taylor had more than once intimated to the War Department that, in his opinion, no such movement was necessary to the defence or protection of Texas.

9. Speech by Representative Alexander Hamilton Stephens, Democrat from Georgia, on February 12, 1847. He was later Vice President

of the Confederacy and Governor of Georgia.[32]

But some gentlemen, who will not directly avow the principle of conquest as the object of the war, yet take the position that territory must be acquired as its result, by way of *indemnity* for what Mexico owes us, and the expenses of the war — that she is unable to pay in money, and territory must be taken. Now, sir, I am equally opposed to this; for how could any of the Mexican territory, so acquired, by possibility be considered an *indemnity?* An indemnity is something to save from loss — something of pecuniary value; but how could these departments of Mexico — California and New Mexico, if you please — converted into American territories or provinces, be of any such value to us? Will you make a Sicily of one, and place it under the praetorship of a Verrer, to exact tribute from the inhabitants, and in this way secure indemnity; and make a Bombay of the other, and place it under the rule of a Hastings, who, by grinding oppression, shall cause annual streams of treasure to flow into your coffers? . . .

10. Letter of F. W. Byrdsall to John C. Calhoun, dated July 19, 1847:[33]

The annexation of Texas with its cotton soil and Anglo-American population was a measure of absolute necessity to the United States; not so the annexation of Mexico with the population she has. It *was* our interest to preserve her republican nationality equally from ourselves and from Europe. But *now* we must take her, in order to keep her from the hands of others, and we will become deteriorated by such a junction morally, while politically

---

[32] *Congressional Globe,* 29th Cong., 2d Sess., Appendix, 353.

[33] J. Franklin Jameson, ed., *Correspondence of John C. Calhoun, 4th Annual Report of the Historical Manuscripts Commission of the A. H. A.* (Washington, 1900), 1127.

the Union of the States will not be strengthened. However we may *want* the lands, we surely do not *need* the incorporation with us of such a people of inferior mixture as the Mexican. We have started upon the course of conquest, we cannot now recede if we would, our success will create circumstances to impel us onward in that direction, whether we are willing or not.

With the accession of several millions of Mexicans at one swoop — with the vast increase of Emigration from all parts of Europe, the question presents itself, can this extensive territory and people ultimately escape the fate all monarchal and Republican Empires have fallen under? Namely dismemberment.

11. Message of Governor Charles Nixon Briggs of Massachusetts, January 11, 1848. Briggs was a prominent Whig leader in the Bay State.[34]

If the result of this war is to be the conquest of the whole, or a large portion of the territory of Mexico, and its annexation to this republic, the consequences to be apprehended from such a result, to the peace and harmony of the people of the United States, are far more appalling than the war itself.

12. Senator Thomas Corwin was a Whig who opposed war with Mexico. In making the following statements in 1847, he injured further political advancement:[35]

Sir, look at this pretence of want of room. With twenty millions of people, you have about one thousand millions of acres of land,

[34] *Niles' National Register,* January 22, 1848, 334.

[35] Albert Bushnell Hart, ed., *American History Told by Contemporaries.* IV, *Welding of the Nation, 1845–1900* (The Macmillan Company, New York, 1901), 25–28.

inviting settlement by every conceivable argument, bringing them down to a quarter of a dollar an acre, and allowing every man to squat where he pleases. But the Senator from Michigan says we will be two hundred millions in a few years, and we want room. If I were a Mexican I would tell you, "Have you not room in your own country to bury your dead men? If you come into mine, we will greet you with bloody hands, and welcome you to hospitable graves."

Why, says the chairman of this Committee on Foreign Relations, it is the most reasonable thing in the world! We ought to have the Bay of San Francisco. Why? Because it is the best harbor on the Pacific! It has been my fortune, Mr. President, to have practised a good deal in criminal courts in the course of my life, but I never yet heard a thief, arraigned for stealing a horse, plead that it was the best horse that he could find in the country! We want California. What for? Why, says the Senator from Michigan, we will have it; and the Senator from South Carolina, with a very mistaken view, I think, of policy, says you can't keep our people from going there. I don't desire to prevent them. Let them go and seek their happiness in whatever country or clime it pleases them.

All I ask of them is, not to require this Government to protect them with that banner consecrated to war waged for principles — eternal, enduring truth. Sir, it is not meet that our old flag should throw its protecting folds over expeditions for lucre or for land. But you still say you want room for your people. This has been the plea of every robber chief from Nimrod to the present hour. . . .

13. Speech by Representative David Wilmot of Pennsylvania, who during the debate over the war introduced his famous proviso on

February 8, 1847, and initiated heated debate:[36]

[THE WILMOT PROVISO]

. . . That there shall be neither slavery nor involuntary servitude in any territory on the continent of America which shall hereafter be acquired by, or annexed to, the United States by virtue of this appropriation, or in any other manner whatever, except for crimes whereof the party shall have been duly convicted. . . .

❋ ❋ ❋ ❋ ❋ ❋

Now, sir, we are told that California is ours; that New Mexico is ours — won by the valor of our arms. They are free. Shall they remain free? Shall these fair provinces be the inheritance and homes of the white labor of freemen or the black labor of slaves? This, sir, is the issue — this the question. The North has the right, and her representatives have the power. Shall the right prevail? I fear not, sir. There is a power more potent than the right. These fair provisions are ours — so held, and so regarded by the Administration. But of this I shall speak more fully hereafter. All we ask is, that their character be preserved. They are now free. It is a general principle of the law of nations, that in conquered or acquired territories, all laws therein existing, not inconsistent with its new allegiance, shall remain in force until altered or repealed. This law prohibits slavery in California and in New Mexico. But the South contend, that in their emigration to this free territory, they have the right to take and hold slaves, the same as other property. Unless the amendment I have offered be adopted, or other early legislation is had upon this subject, they will do so. . . .

[36] *Congressional Globe*, 29th Cong., 2d Sess., Appendix, 149–150, 315.

14. Speech by Representative Charles Hudson, Whig from Massachusetts, on February 13, 1847:[37]

I tell you, Mr. Chairman, that the North will stand firm. You cannot judge of the present by the past. Within two years there has been a radical change in public sentiment in the free States. The Texas outrage, followed by this iniquitous war, both for the extension of slavery, has brought the people to their senses. From the State of Maine, from the granite hills of New Hampshire, from united New England, the word has gone forth, and the glorious response from New York, from Pennsylvania, from Ohio, leaves no doubt on the subject of public feeling. The sentiment is deep-rooted; it is a strong religious conviction that slavery is a curse, and is at war with the best interests of our country and of humanity. A great moral revolution has commenced, and such revolutions can never go backward. They have seen this administration breaking through the barriers of the Constitution to sustain and extend slavery, and the people in the free States have resolved that the evil shall extend no farther. I say to the South in all frankness, you will find Northern sentiment immovable on the subject, "as firm as nature, and as fixed as fate." And I will say to these Democrats of the North, who are fawning around this weak administration, and betraying northern interests, they may pick the crumbs which fall from the Executive table — you are treasuring up for yourselves wrath against the day of wrath. . . .

15. Speech by Representative William W. Wick, Democrat from Indiana, on February 2, 1847:[38]

Sir, the Wilmot proviso is a bird of ill omen. I seek not to

[37] *Ibid.*, 369–370.
[38] *Ibid.*, 159, 160.

arraign the motives of its advocates. But it is a truce-breaker — a disturber of legislative peace on the floor of Congress — and therefore I am against it. It is introduced out of time, and out of place, and therefore I am against it.

There is no necessity *now* for acting upon the subject contemplated by it, and therefore I am against it.

The effect of this measure which is so often mentioned, is well understood here; but it may be otherwise elsewhere. It assumes what may, or may not, turn out to be correct; to-wit, that in one way or another, we are about to acquire territory heretofore and yet belonging to Mexico, though now wholly, or in part, in our military possession; and it declares that neither slavery nor involuntary servitude shall ever exist in such territory.

The effect of bringing forward this measure is to excite here heated debates on the abstract question of slavery, at a season when the time of the national legislature would be better appropriated to the consideration of providing the ways and means, money, men, and munitions, for bringing the war to a speedy and successful close. By promoting worldly strife here, it is calculated to waste precious time; and by promoting sectional jealousies, and heart-burnings, it is calculated to drown our high sense of patriotism, and lead us to forget our foreign foes, in our resentments against those we may consider as foes at home. Hence it is a disturber of the peace. . . .

16. A popular school history textbook of the 1860's contained the following account:[39]

Such was the conclusion of the Mexican war, — a war opposed as impolitic and unjust by one portion of the American people,

[39] Marcius Willson, *History of the United States*, . . . Revised and illustrated edition (Ivison, Phinney & Co., New York, 1860), 361–362.

and as cordially approved by the other, but admitted by all to have established for our nation, by the unbroken series of brilliant victories won by our army, a character for martial heroism which knows no superior in the annals of history, and which fears no rivals in the pathway of military glory. But war is seldom without its alloy of bitterness; and in this instance it was not alone its ordinary calamities of suffering, and wretchedness, and death, — the "sighs of orphans, and widows' tears," — that moderated our exultations; but with our very rejoicings were mingled the deep and sullen notes of discord; and with the laurels of victory, with which fame had encircled the brow of our nation's glory, were entwined the cypress and the yew — emblems of mourning.

The vast extent of unoccupied territory which we had acquired as the result of the conquest, proved an apple of discord in our midst; and the question of the final disposal of the prize was a problem which our profoundest statesmen found it difficult to solve. The South and the North took issue upon it — the former claiming the right of her citizens to remove, with their property in slaves, on to any lands purchased by the common treasure of the republic, and the latter demanding that territory free from slavery at the time of its acquisition, should for ever remain so.

17. The Treaty of Guadalupe Hidalgo, 1848.[40]

ARTICLE I.

There shall be firm and universal peace between the United States of America and the Mexican Republic, and between their respective countries, territories, cities, towns and people, without exception of places or persons.

[40] Hunter Miller, ed., *Treaties and Other International Acts of the United States of America*, V (United States Government Printing Office, Washington, 1937), 213–214, 222.

* * * * * *

ARTICLE V.

The Boundary line between the two Republics shall commence in the Gulf of Mexico, three leagues from land, opposite the mouth of the Rio Grande, otherwise called Río Bravo del Norte, or opposite the mouth of its deepest branch, if it should have more than one branch emptying directly into the sea; from thence, up the middle of that river, following the deepest channel . . . to the point where it strikes the southern boundary of New Mexico; thence, westwardly, along the whole southern boundary of New Mexico (which runs north of the town called *Paso*) to its western termination; thence, northward, along the western line of New Mexico, until it intersects the first branch of the river Gila; . . . thence down the middle of the said branch of the said river, until it empties into the Rio Colorado, thence across the Rio Colorado, following the division line between Upper and Lower California, to the Pacific Ocean. . . .

. . . And, in order to preclude all difficulty in tracing upon the ground the limit separating Upper and Lower California, it is agreed that the said limit shall consist of a straight line, drawn from the middle of the Rio Gila, where it unites with the Colorado, to a point on the coast of the Pacific Ocean, distant one marine league due south of the southernmost point of the Port of San Diego. . . .

* * * * * *

ARTICLE XII.

In consideration of the extension acquired by the boundaries of the United States, as defined in the fifth Article of the present Treaty, the Government of the United States engages to pay to that of the Mexican Republic the sum of fifteen Millions of Dollars.

18. An 1850 Mexican version of American expansion.[41]

The North American Republic has already absorbed territories pertaining to Great Britain, France, Spain, and Mexico. It has employed every means to accomplish this — purchase as well as usurpation, skill as well as force, and nothing has restrained it when treating of territorial acquisition. Louisiana, the Floridas, Oregon, and Texas, have successively fallen into its power. It now has secured the possession of the Californias, New Mexico, and a great part of other States and Territories of the Mexican Republic. Although we may desire to close our eyes with the assurances that these pretentions have now come to an end, and that we may enjoy peace and unmoved tranquility for a long time, still the past history has an abundance of matter to teach us as yet existing, what has existed, the same schemes of conquest in the United States. The attempt has to be made, and we will see ourselves overwhelmed anew, sooner or later, in another or in more than one disastrous war, until the flag of the stars floats over the last span of territory which it so much covets. . . .

A short time before the independence of Mexico, in the year 1819, the Spanish government granted to Moses Austin the requisite authority to form a colony in Texas. This concession was owing principally to the zeal that animated the King of Spain for the dissemination and protection of the Catholic religion. Moses Austin had represented his sect as disheartened and dispersed, and begged that these lands might be given to him as an asylum, where the immigrants could and would enter for the exercise of their faith.

---

[41] Albert C. Ramsey, ed., *The Other Side: or Notes for the History of the War between Mexico and the United States. Written in Mexico. Translated from the Spanish* (John Wiley, New York, 1850), 3–4, 15–16, 18–19, 30–31.

Stephen Austin, the son and heir of Moses, continued the work commenced by his father, and made a beginning of a vast enterprise by colonizing, in 1820, between the Brasos and Colorado rivers. The emancipation of our Republic opened a wide door to immigration. They received with open arms the strangers who touched our soil. But the political inexperience of our national governors converted into a fountain of evils a benevolent and purely Christian principle. Immigration, which ought to have equalized the laborious arms to agriculture, manufacture, and commerce, finally resulted in the separation of one of the most important states. It was this which involved us soon in actual, disastrous war.

The object which we aim at is to show that the United States intended to obtain this territory at any price; and to accomplish it, introduced there her citizens, taking care to increase the population. Whereby, already in the year 1829, they counted 20,000 inhabitants in that part [Texas] where formerly they had 3,000. Their minds were prepared gradually to embrace the first opportunity that might offer to strike the blow. . . .

The [Mexican] Republic could not remain indifferent to the cry of rebellion raised within her borders. It endeavored to have order restored in the department in a state of revolt, trying in the first place the conciliatory method of agreement [with the rebelling Texans]. It proposed to the colonies new advantages, and franchises; among others, that of being exempt for another period of ten years from paying taxes. When it was seen only that every peaceable proposition was discarded, it was decided to declare war [on the Texans], and subject, by actual force, those who were not willing to hear any other argument than the roar of the cannon. The army marched upon Texas; General Santa

Anna placed himself at its head; and the campaign opened under the most favorable circumstances.

The Texans, on their side, prepared to make a vigorous resistance. To sustain it they counted on effectual aid from the United States, which gave protection to them, — covert, indeed, but still decided and constant. Supplies for the war, arms, men, and whatever was requisite, left the most populous cities . . . [of the United States] to assist the cause of the Texans, while it protested that it observed the most strict neutrality. The whole world witnessed the conduct pursued by the American government, which could do no less than discover the plans which it proposed. . . .

To explain the occupation of the Mexican territory by the troops of General Taylor, the strange idea occurred to the United States that the limits of Texas extended to the Río Bravo del Norte [the Rio Grande]. This opinion was predicated upon two distinct principles: one, that the Congress of Texas had so declared it in December, in 1836; and another, that the river mentioned had been the natural line of Louisiana [as mentioned in the Louisiana Purchase of 1803]. To state these reasons is equivalent at once to deciding the matter; for no one could defend such . . . absurdities. The first, which this [Texan] government . . . supported . . . would have been ridiculous in the mouth of a child. Whom could it convince that the declaration of the Texas Congress bore a legal title for the acquisition of the lands which it appropriated to itself with so little hesitation? If such a principle were recognized, we ought to be very grateful to these gentlemen senators who had the kindness to be satisfied with so little. Why not declare the limits of the rebel state [Texas] extended to . . . the capital [Mexico City], or to our frontier with Guatemala?

The question is so clear in itself that it would only obscure by delaying to examine it further. We pass then to the other no less nonsensical than the former. In the first place to pretend that the limits of Louisiana came to the Río Bravo, it was essential to confound this province with Texas, which never can be tolerated. In the beginning of this article we have already shown the ancient and peaceable possession of Spain over the lands of the latter. Again, this same province, and afterwards State of Texas, never had extended its territory to the Río Bravo, being only the Nueces, in which always had been established the boundary. Lastly, a large part of the territory situated on the other side of the Bravo, belonged, without dispute or doubt, to other states of the Republic — to New Mexico, Tamaulipas, Coahuila, and Chihuahua [Mexican states].

IV

THE ROLE OF AN IDEA
IN HISTORY

In this part you will encounter later observations about the role of an idea in history. As you read them, ask yourself: Does an idea make history? Does an idea emerge from history as a rationalization of what people do for other reasons?

1. Carl Schurz was a German-born reformer and prominent Republican. In 1898 he had opposed United States acquisition of the Philippines after the defeat of Spain in the Spanish-American War. Six years before, he voiced the following sentiments about American interests in the Pacific.[1]

Whenever there is a project on foot to annex foreign territory to this republic the cry of "manifest destiny" is raised to produce the impression that all opposition to such a project is a struggle against fate. . . .

* * * * * *

The new "manifest-destiny" precept means, in point of principle, not merely the incorporation in the United States of territory contiguous to our borders, but rather the acquisition of such territory, far and near, as may be useful in enlarging our commercial advantages, and in securing to our navy facilities desirable for the operations of a great naval power. . . .

[1] Carl Schurz, "Manifest Destiny," *Harper's New Monthly Magazine,* LXXXCII (October, 1893), No. DXXI, 737, 738, 745–746.

* * * * * *

The advocates of the annexation policy advance some arguments which require but a passing notice. They say that unless we take a certain country offered to us — Hawaii, for instance — some other power will take it, and that, having refused ourselves, we cannot object. This is absurd. Having shown ourselves unselfish, we shall have all the greater moral authority in objecting to an arrangement which would be obnoxious to our interests.

We are told that unless we take charge of a certain country it will be ill-governed and get into internal trouble. This is certainly no inducement. This republic cannot take charge of all countries that are badly governed. On the contrary, a country apt to get into internal trouble would be no desirable addition to our national household.

We are told that the people of a certain country wish to join us, and it would be wrong to repel them. But the question whether a stranger is to be admitted as a member of our family it is our right and our duty to decide according to our own view of the family interest.

2. Woodrow Wilson was President of the United States from 1913 to 1921. In an article entitled "The Ideals of America," Wilson stated in 1902:[2]

There sprang up the lusty states which now, in these days of our full stature, outnumber almost threefold the thirteen commonwealths which formed the Union. Their growth set the pace of our life; forced the slavery question to a final issue; gave us the civil war with its stupendous upheaval and its resettlement of the very foundations of the government; spread our strength from

2 Woodrow Wilson, "The Ideals of America," *The Atlantic Monthly*, XC (December, 1902), 726.

142

sea to sea; created us a free and mighty people, whose destinies daunt the imagination of the Old World looking on. That increase, that endless accretion, that rolling, resistless tide, incalculable in its strength, infinite in its variety, has made us what we are; has put the resources of a huge continent at our disposal; has provoked us to invention and given us mighty captains of industry. This great pressure of a people moving always to new frontiers, in search of new lands, new power, the full freedom of a virgin world, has ruled our course and formed our policies like a Fate. It gave us, not Louisiana alone, but Florida also. It forced war with Mexico upon us, and gave us the coasts of the Pacific. It swept Texas into the Union. It made for Alaska a territory of the United States. Who shall say where it will end?

3. Henry Nash Smith is a noted authority on the American West. In describing the expansion of the 19th century, he declared:[3]

. . . But one of the most persistent generalizations concerning American life and character is the notion that our society has been shaped by the pull of a vacant continent drawing population westward through the passes of the Alleghenies, across the Mississippi Valley, over the high plains and mountains of the Far West to the Pacific Coast.

❋   ❋   ❋   ❋   ❋   ❋

The early visions of an American Empire embody two different if often mingled conceptions. There is on the one hand the notion of empire as command of the sea, and on the other hand the notion of empire as a populous future society occupying the

[3] Henry Nash Smith, *Virgin Land: The American West as Symbol and Myth* (Vintage Books, Inc., New York, 1959), 3, 13.

interior of the American continent. If these two kinds of empire are not mutually exclusive — for we can readily concede that patriots would want to claim every separate glory for their country — they nevertheless rest on different economic bases and imply different policies. Engrossing the trade of the world is an ambition evidently taken over from the British mercantilist ideal. On the other hand, creating new states in the dreary solitudes of the West is an enterprise that depends upon the increase of population resulting from agricultural expansion into an empty, fertile continent. This second version of the American Empire, based on agrarian assumptions, more nearly corresponds to the actual course of events during the nineteenth century.

Both these conceptions predict the outcome of the westward movement. Empire conceived as maritime dominion presupposes American expansion westward to the Pacific. The idea draws upon the long history and rich overtones of the search for a northwest passage to Asia, or, in Whitman's phrase, a "passage to India." . . . The hunter and trapper who served as the pathfinder of overland expansion and became one of the fixtures of American mythology forms the subject of [the sons of leatherstocking]. . . . The very different idea of a continental empire dependent upon agriculture and associated with various images of the Good Society to be realized in the West, may be called the theme of the Garden of the World. . . .

4. Richard Hofstadter is a noted scholar and writer of American history. In his interpretation of the agrarian myth he wrote:[4]

Like any complex of ideas, the agrarian myth cannot be defined in a phrase, but its component themes form a clear pattern. Its

[4] Richard Hofstadter, *The Age of Reform, from Bryan to F.D.R.* (Vintage Books, 1961, published by Alfred A. Knopf, Inc., New York, 1955), 24–25.

hero was the yeoman farmer, its central conception the notion that he is the ideal man and the ideal citizen. Unstinted praise of the special virtues of the farmer and the special values of rural life was coupled with the assertion that agriculture, as a calling uniquely productive and uniquely important to society, had a special right to the concern and protection of government. The yeoman, who owned a small farm and worked it with the aid of his family, was the incarnation of the simple, honest, independent, healthy, happy human being. Because he lived in close communion with beneficent nature, his life was believed to have a wholesomeness and integrity impossible for the depraved populations of cities. His well-being was not merely physical, it was moral; it was not merely personal, it was the central source of civic virtue; it was not merely secular but religious, for God had made the land and called man to cultivate it. Since the yeoman was believed to be both happy and honest, and since he had a secure propertied stake in society in the form of his own land, he was held to be the best and most reliable sort of citizen. To this conviction Jefferson appealed when he wrote: "The small land holders are the most precious part of a state."

[Hofstadter defined the term "myth" as:]

By "myth" as I use the word here, I do not mean an idea that is simply false, but rather one that so effectively embodies men's values that it profoundly influences their way of perceiving reality and hence their behavior. In this sense myths may have varying degrees of fiction or reality. The agrarian myth became increasingly fictional as time went on.

5. Walter Lippmann, a critic of this century, on the use of a symbol wrote:[5]

When political parties or newspapers declare for Americanism, Progressivism, Law and Order, Justice, Humanity, they hope to amalgamate the emotions or conflicting factions which would surely divide, if, instead of these symbols, they were invited to discuss a specific program. For when a coalition around the symbol has been effected, feeling flows toward conformity under the symbol rather than toward critical scrutiny of the measures. It is, I think, convenient and technically correct to call multiple phrases like these symbolic. They do not stand for specific ideas, but for a sort of truce or junction between ideas. They are like a strategic railroad center where many roads converge regardless of their ultimate origin or their ultimate destination. But he who captures the symbols by which public feeling is for the moment contained, controls by that much the approaches of public policy. And as long as a particular symbol has the power of coalition, ambitious factions will fight for possession. Think, for example, of Lincoln's name or of Theodore Roosevelt's. A leader or an interest that can make itself master of current symbols is master of the current situation. . . .

[5] Walter Lippmann, *Public Opinion* (Harcourt, Brace and Company, New York, 1922), 206–207.

Chronology

1841 — Mar. 4   Inauguration of President William Henry Harrison.

Apr. 4   Death of President Harrison. John Tyler became President.

1842 — Aug. 20   The Webster-Ashburton Treaty with Great Brittain settled a dispute over the northeastern boundary of the United States.

Aug.   John C. Frémont explored the South Pass in the Rocky Mountains.

1843 — Sept.   Frémont explored the Great Salt Lake.

1844 — July 7   Joseph Smith, the Mormon prophet, killed by a mob in Carthage, Illinois. Mormons began to plan for migration to Utah.

1845 — Jan. 16   United States ratified a treaty for trade with China.

Feb. 28   Congress passed a joint resolution to annex Texas.

Mar. 1   President Tyler signed the joint resolution for the annexation of Texas.

Mar. 3   Congress admitted the states of Iowa and Florida into the Union.

Mar. 4   Inauguration of President James K. Polk.

Mar.   Frémont sent with an armed party of 63 to California.

July 30   General Zachary Taylor ordered into Texas.

1846 — Jan. 13   General Taylor ordered to the mouth of the Rio Grande River.

Apr. 23   Mexico declares war against the United States.

May 11   President Polk's message informed Congress that the Mexican War had begun.

May 13	Congress declared war against Mexico.
June 16	Treaty between the United States and Great Britain settled the northern boundary of Oregon.
July 6	Americans in California under Frémont's leadership declared independence.
1847 — Sept. 14	Mexico captured by American troops. Wilmot Proviso defeated in Congress.
1848 — Jan.	Gold discovered in California.
Feb. 2	Treaty of peace with Mexico signed at Guadalupe-Hidalgo.
Feb. 22	Treaty of Guadalupe-Hidalgo submitted by President Polk to the Senate for its approval.
Feb. 23	Death of John Quincy Adams.
May 29	Wisconsin admitted into the Union as a state.
Aug. 13	Oregon made a territory of the United States.
1849 — Mar. 3	Minnesota made a territory of the United States.
Mar. 4	Inauguration of President Zachary Taylor.
1850 — July 9	Death of President Taylor. Millard Fillmore became President.
Sept.	The Compromise of 1850. By its terms:

1. California became a free state.
2. Utah and New Mexico became territories. The question of slavery was to be decided by vote of the actual inhabitants.
3. Texas received $10,000,000 as compensation for surrendering its claim to lands at its western limits.
4. The slave trade was abolished in the District of Columbia.
5. A new and more strict fugitive slave law was passed.

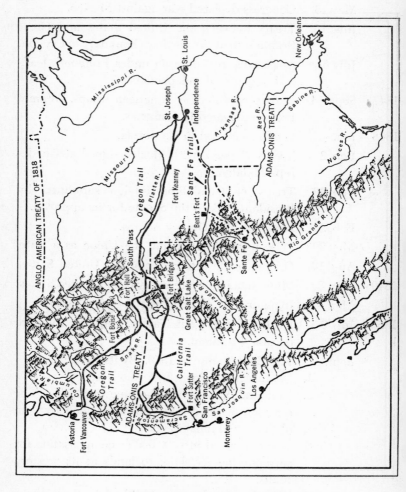

THE WEST IN THE 1840's

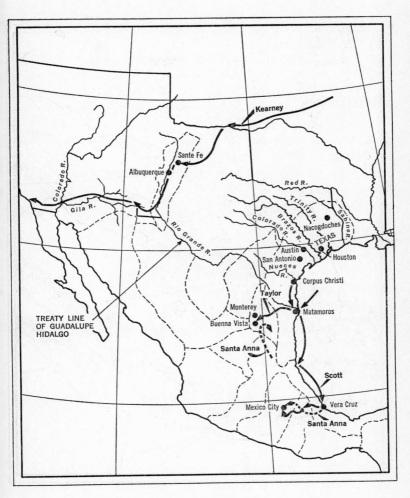

MEXICAN TERRITORY

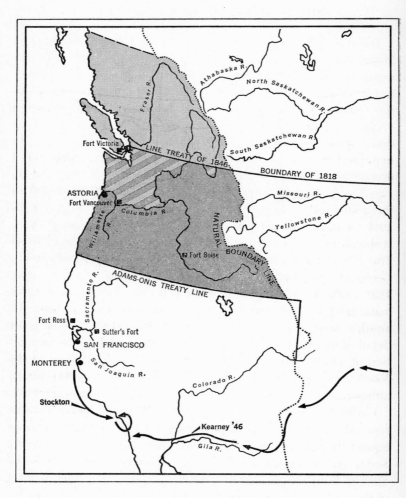

THE FAR WEST

Suggested Additional Reading

The standard work on Manifest Destiny is Albert K. Weinberg's *Manifest Destiny* (Baltimore, 1935), a broad survey of American expansionism and the American idea of a mission from its intellectual origins to the twentieth century. Frederick Merk's *Manifest Destiny and Mission in American History: A Reinterpretation* (New York, 1963) regards as a more valid expression of the national spirit in 1846, not Manifest Destiny but mission — an all-important mission as idealistic, self-denying, and hopeful of a divine favor. Bernard De Voto's *The Year of Decision, 1846* (Boston, 1943) is a lively source about migrations westward in the 1840's. Otis A. Singletary's *The Mexican War* (Chicago, 1960) is mainly an account of military operations of the conflict. It should be compared with the more comprehensive two-volume *The War with Mexico* (New York, 1919) by Justin H. Smith. George L. Rives's two-volume *The United States and Mexico, 1821–1848* (New York, 1913) deals with the maze of early diplomatic relations between the United States and Mexico. Justin H. Smith's *Annexation of Texas* (New York, 1911) tells in great detail of the various maneuvers finally culminating in the annexation of Texas. Hubert H. Bancroft's two-volume *History of the North American States and Texas* (San Francisco, 1884–1889), although old, still provides much material on the Texas question.

Carlos E. Casteñeda's *The Mexican Side of the Texas Revolution* (Dallas, 1928) is an account of what some leading Mexican figures thought of the Texan revolt. The Chronicles of America Series has several works available. Herbert E. Bolton's *The Spanish Borderlands* (New Haven, 1921) provides a brief account of the exploration and settlement of the Southwest. Nathaniel W. Stephenson's *Texas and the Mexican War* (New Haven, 1921) is a general survey of events from the era of Stephen F. Austin through the Treaty of Guadalupe Hidalgo. Constance L. Skinner's *Adventures of Oregon* (New Haven, 1920) is a general account of events in Oregon from the Lewis and Clark expedition through the story of Marcus Whitman. Stewart Edward White's *The Forty-Niners* (New Haven, 1918) deals primarily with the motives of those who migrated to California and the results of such a migration. Eugene C. Barker's *Mexico and Texas, 1821–1835* (Dallas, 1928) provides some insight into the background of the Texas Revolution. It should be compared to William C. Brinkley's *The Texas Revolution* (Baton Rouge, 1952). E. D. Adams' *British Interests and Activities in Texas, 1838–1846* (Baltimore, 1910) is just what the title implies. Norman A. Graebner's *Empire on the Pacific* (New York, 1955) supports the argument that commercial interests looking to the potential Pacific trade were a cause of the Mexican War. An excellent source for further identification of congressmen involved in the events of the 1840's is the *Biographical Directory of the American Congress, 1774–1961, House Document No. 442*, 85th Congress, 2nd Session (1961). Other sources can be found in *The Harvard Guide to American History* (Cambridge, Massachusetts, 1954) and in the bibliographies of Samuel F. Bemis' *A Diplomatic History of the United States* (New York, 1950) and Thomas A. Bailey's *A Diplomatic History of the American People* (New York, 1955).

1 2 3 4 5 6 7 8 9 0